FREDERIK POHL

THE MAN WHO ATE
THE WORLD

BALLANTINE BOOKS   NEW YORK

BALLANTINE BOOKS, INC.
101 Fifth Avenue, New York 3, N. Y.

CONTENTS

THE MAN WHO ATE THE WORLD

I

He had a name, but at home he was called "Sonny," and he was almost always at home. He hated it. Other boys his age went to school. Sonny would have done anything to go to school, but his family was, to put it mildly, not well off. It wasn't Sonny's fault that his father was spectacularly unsuccessful. But it meant—no school for Sonny, no boys of his own age for Sonny to play with. All childhoods are tragic (as all adults forget), but Sonny's was misery all the way through.

The worst time was at night, when the baby sister was asleep and the parents were grimly eating and reading and dancing and drinking, until they were ready to drop. And of all bad nights, the night before his twelfth birthday was perhaps Sonny's worst. He was old enough to know what a birthday party was like. It would be cake and candy, shows and games; it would be presents, presents, presents. It would be a terrible, endless day.

He switched off the color-D television and the recorded tapes of sea chanteys and, with an appearance of absent-mindedness, walked toward the door of his playroom.

Davey Crockett got up from beside the model rocket field and said, "Hold on thar, Sonny. Mought take a stroll with you." Davey's face was serene and strong as a Tennessee crag; it swung its long huntin' rifle under one arm and put its other arm around Sonny's shoulders. "Where you reckon we ought to head?"

Sonny shook Davey Crockett's arm off. "Get lost," he said petulantly. "Who wants you around?"

Long John Silver came out of the closet, hobbling on its wooden leg, crouched over its knobby cane. "Ah, young master," it said reproachfully, "you shouldn't ought to talk to old Davey like that! He's a good friend to you, Davey is. Many's the weary day Davey and me has been a-keepin' of your company. I asks you this, young master: Is it fair and square that you should be a-tellin' him to get lost? Is it fair, young master? Is it square?"

Sonny looked at the floor stubbornly and didn't answer. My gosh, what was the use of answering dummies like them? He stood rebelliously silent and still until he just felt like saying something. And then he said: "You go in the closet, both of you. I don't want to play with you. I'm going to play with my trains."

Long John said unctuously, "Now there's a good idea, that is! You just be a-havin' of a good time with your trains, and old Davey and me'll——"

"Go ahead!" shouted Sonny. He stood stamping his foot until they were out of sight.

His fire truck was in the middle of the floor; he kicked at it, but it rolled quickly out of reach and slid into its little garage under the tanks of tropical fish. He scuffed over to the model railroad layout and glared at it. As he approached, the Twentieth Century Limited came roaring out of a tunnel, sparks flying from its stack. It crossed a bridge, whistled at a grade crossing, steamed into the Union Station. The roof of the station glowed and suddenly became transparent, and through it Sonny saw the bustling crowds of redcaps and travelers—

"I don't want that," he said. "Casey, crack up old Number Ninety-Nine again."

Obediently the layout quivered and revolved a half-turn. Old Casey Jones, one and an eighth inches tall, leaned out of the cab of the S.P. locomotive and waved good-by to Sonny. The locomotive whistled shrilly twice and started to pick up speed—

It was a good crackup. Little old Casey's body, thrown completely free, developed real blisters from the steam and bled real blood. But Sonny turned his back on it. He had liked that crackup for a long time—longer than he liked almost any other toy he owned. But he was tired of it.

He looked around the room.

Tarzan of the Apes, leaning against a foot-thick tree trunk, one hand on a vine, lifted its head and looked at him. But Tarzan, Sonny calculated craftily, was clear across the room. The others were in the closet—

Sonny ran out and slammed the door. He saw Tarzan start to come after him, but even before Sonny was out of the room Tarzan slumped and stood stock-still.

It wasn't fair, Sonny thought angrily. It wasn't fair! They wouldn't even *chase* him, so that at least he could have some kind of chance to get away by himself. They'd just talk to each other on their little radios, and in a minute one of the tutors, or one of the maids, or whatever else happened to be handy, would vector in on him. And that would be that.

But for the moment he was free.

He slowed down and walked down the Great Hall toward his baby sister's room. The fountains began to splash as he entered the hall; the mosaics on the wall began to tinkle music and sparkle with moving colors.

"Now, chile, whut you up to!"

He turned around, but he knew it was Mammy coming toward him. It was slapping toward him on big, flat feet, its pink-palmed hands lifted to its shoulders. The face under the red bandanna was frowning, the gold tooth sparkling as it scolded: "Chile, you is got us'n's so worried we's fit to *die!* How you 'speck us to take good keer of you ef'n you run off lak that? Now you jes come on back to your nice room with Mammy an' we'll see if there ain't some real nice program on the teevee."

Sonny stopped and waited for it, but he wouldn't give it the satisfaction of looking at it. Slap-slap the big feet waddled cumbersomely toward him; but he didn't have any illusions. Waddle, big feet, three hundred pounds and all, Mammy could catch him in twenty yards with a ten-yard start. Any of them could.

He said in his best icily indignant voice, "I was just going in to look at my baby sister."

Pause. "You was?" The plump black face looked suspicious.

"Yes, I was. Doris is my very own sister, and I love her very much."

Pause—long pause. "Dat's nice," said Mammy, but its voice was still doubtful. "I 'speck I better come 'long with you. You wouldn't want to wake your lil baby sister up. Ef I come I'll he'p you keep real quiet."

Sonny shook free of it—they were always putting their hands on you! "I don't *want* you to come with me, Mammy!"

"Aw now, honey! Mammy ain't gwine bother nothin', you knows that."

Sonny turned his back on it and marched grimly toward his sister's room. If only they would leave him *alone!* But they never did. It was always that way, always one darn old robot—yes, *robot*, he thought, savagely tasting the naughty word. Always one darn *robot* after another. Why couldn't Daddy be like other daddies, so they could live in a decent little house and get rid of these darn *robots*—so he could go to a real school and be in a class with other boys, instead of being taught at home by Miss Brooks and Mr. Chips and all those other *robots?*

They spoiled everything. And they would spoil what he wanted to do now. But he was going to do it all the same, because there was something in Doris's room that he wanted very much.

It was probably the only tangible thing he wanted in the world.

As they passed the imitation tumbled rocks of the Bear Cave, Mama Bear poked its head out and growled: "Hello, Sonny. Don't you think you ought to be in bed? It's nice and warm in our bear bed, Sonny."

He didn't even look at it. Time was when he had liked that sort of thing too, but he wasn't a four-year-old like Doris any more. All the same, there was one thing a four-year-old had—

He stopped at the door of her room. "Doris?" he whispered.

Mammy scolded: "Now, chile, you knows that lil baby is asleep! How come you tryin' to wake her up?"

"I won't wake her up." The farthest thing from Sonny's mind was to wake his sister up. He tiptoed into the room and stood beside the little girl's bed. Lucky kid! he thought enviously. Being four, she was allowed to have a tiny little room and a tiny bed—where Sonny had to wallow around in a forty-foot bedchamber and a bed eight feet long.

He looked down at his sister. Behind him Mammy clucked approvingly. "Dat's nice when chilluns loves each other lak you an' that lil baby," it whispered.

Doris was sound asleep, clutching her teddy-bear. It wriggled slightly and opened an eye to look at Sonny, but it didn't say anything.

Sonny took a deep breath, leaned forward and gently slipped the teddy-bear out of the bed.

It scrambled pathetically, trying to get free. Behind him Mammy whispered urgently: "Sonny! Now you let dat ole teddy-bear alone, you heah me?"

Sonny whispered, "I'm not hurting anything. Leave me alone, will you?"

"Sonny!"

He clutched the little furry robot desperately around its middle. The stubby arms pawed at him, the furred feet scratched against his arms. It growled a tiny doll-bear growl, and whined, and suddenly his hands were wet with its real salt tears.

"Sonny! Come on now, honey, you knows that's Doris's teddy. Aw, chile!"

He said, "It's mine!" It wasn't his. He knew it wasn't his. His was long gone, taken away from him when he was six because it was *old*, and because he had been six and six-year-olds had to have bigger, more elaborate companion-robots. It wasn't even the same color as his—it was brown, where his had been black and white. But it was cuddly and gently warm; and he had heard it whispering little make-believe bedtime stories to Doris. And he wanted it, very much.

Footsteps in the hall outside. A low-pitched pleading voice from the door: "Sonny, you must not interfere with your sister's toys. One has obligations."

He stood forlornly, holding the teddy-bear. "Go away, Mr. Chips!"

"Really, Sonny! This isn't proper behavior. Please return the toy."

He cried: "I won't!"

Mammy, dark face pleading in the shadowed room, leaned toward him and tried to take it away from him. "Aw, honey, now you knows dat's not——"

"Leave me alone!" he shouted. There was a gasp and a little cry from the bed, and Doris sat up and began to weep.

Well, they had their way. The little girl's bedroom was suddenly filled with robots—and not only robots, for in a moment the butler robot appeared, its face stern and sorrowful, leading Sonny's actual flesh-and-blood mother and father. Sonny made a terrible scene. He cried, and he swore at them childishly for being the unsuccessful clods they were; and they nearly wept too, because they were aware that their lack of standing was bad for the children.

But he couldn't keep the teddy.

They got it away from him and marched him back to his room, where his father lectured him while his mother stayed behind to watch Mammy comfort the little girl. His father said: "Sonny, you're a big boy now. We aren't as well off as other people, but you have to help us. Don't you know that, Sonny? We all have to do our part. Your mother and I'll be up till midnight now, consuming, because you've interrupted us with this scene. Can't you at least *try* to consume something bigger than a teddy-bear? It's all right for Doris because she's so little, but a big boy like you——"

"I hate you!" cried Sonny, and he turned his face to the wall.

They punished him, naturally. The first punishment was that they gave him an extra birthday party the week following.

The second punishment was even worse.

II

Later—much, much later, nearly a score of years—a man named Roger Garrick in a place named Fisherman's Island walked into his hotel room.

The light didn't go on.

The bellhop apologized. "We're sorry, sir. We'll have it attended to, if possible."

"If possible?" Garrick's eyebrows went up. The bellhop made putting in a new light tube sound like a major industrial operation. "All right." He waved the bellhop out of the room. It bowed and closed the door.

Garrick looked around him, frowning. One light tube more or less didn't make an awful lot of difference; there was still the light from the sconces at the walls, from the reading lamps at the chairs and chaise longue and from the photomural on the long side of the room—to say nothing of the fact that it was broad, hot daylight outside and light poured through the windows. All the same, it was a new sensation to be in a room where the central lighting wasn't on. He didn't like it. It was—creepy.

A rap on the door. A girl was standing there, young, attractive, rather small. But a woman grown, it was apparent. "Mr. Garrick? Mr. Roosenburg is expecting you on the sun deck."

"All right." He rummaged around in the pile of luggage, looking for his briefcase. It wasn't even sorted out! The bellhop had merely dumped the lot and left.

The girl said, "Is that what you're looking for?" He looked where she was pointing; it was his briefcase, behind another bag. "You'll get used to that around here. Nothing in the right place, nothing working right. We've all got used to it."

We. He looked at her sharply, but she was no robot; there was life, not the glow of electronic tubes, in her eyes. "Pretty bad, is it?"

She shrugged. "Let's go see Mr. Roosenburg. I'm Kathryn Pender, by the way. I'm his statistician."

He followed her out into the hall. "Statistician?"

She turned and smiled—a tight, grim smile of annoyance. "That's right. Surprised?"

Garrick said slowly, "Well, it's more a robot job. Of course, I'm not familiar with the practice in this sector. . . ."

"You will be," she said shortly. "No, we aren't taking the elevator. Mr. Roosenburg's in a hurry to see you."

"But——"

She turned and glared at him. "Don't you understand?
Day before yesterday I took the elevator, and I was hung
up between floors for an hour and a half. Something was
going on at North Guardian, and it took all the power
in the lines. Would it happen again today? I don't know.
But, believe me, an hour and a half is a long time to be
hanging in an elevator." She turned and led him to the
fire stairs. Over her shoulder she said: "Get it straight
once and for all, Mr. Garrick. You're in a disaster area
here. . . . Anyway, it's only ten more flights."

Ten flights.

Nobody climbed ten flights of stairs any more! Garrick
was huffing and puffing before they were halfway, but
the girl kept on ahead, light as a gazelle. Her skirt cut
midway between hip and knees, and Garrick had plenty
of opportunity to observe that her legs were attractively
tanned. Even so, he couldn't help looking around him.
It was a robot's-eye view of the hotel that he was getting;
this was the bare wire armature that held up the con-
fectionery suites and halls where the humans went. Garrick knew, as everyone absent-mindedly knew, that there
were places like this behind the scenes everywhere.
Belowstairs the robots worked; behind scenes, they
moved about their errands and did their jobs. But nobody *went* there. It was funny about the backs of this
girl's knees; they were paler than the rest of the leg—

Garrick wrenched his mind back to his surroundings.
Take the guard rail along the steps, for instance. It was
wire-thin, frail-looking. No doubt it could bear any
weight it was required to, but why couldn't it look that
way? The answer, obviously, was that robots did not
have humanity's built-in concepts of how strong a rail
should look before they could believe it really was
strong. If a robot should be in any doubt—and how im-
probable, that a robot should be in doubt!—it would
perhaps reach out a sculptured hand and test it. Once.
And then it would remember, and never doubt again;
and it wouldn't be continually edging toward the wall,
away from the spider-strand between him and the verti-
cal drop—

He conscientiously took the middle of the steps all the rest of the way up.

Of course that merely meant a different distraction, when he really wanted to do some thinking. But it was a pleasurable distraction. And by the time they reached the top he had solved the problem; the pale spots at the back of Miss Pender's knees meant she had got her suntan the hard way—walking in the sun, perhaps working in the sun, so that the bending knees kept the sun from the patches at the back; not, as anyone else would acquire a tan, by lying beneath a normal, healthful sunlamp held by a robot masseur.

He wheezed: "You don't mean we're all the way up?"

"All the way up," she agreed, and looked at him closely. "Here, lean on me if you want to."

"No, thanks!" He staggered over to the door, which opened naturally enough as he approached it, and stepped out into the flood of sunlight on the roof, to meet Mr. Roosenburg.

Garrick wasn't a medical doctor, but he remembered enough of his basic pre-specialization to know there was something in that fizzy golden drink. It tasted perfectly splendid—just cold enough, just fizzy enough, not quite too sweet. And after two sips of it he was buoyant with strength and well-being.

He put the glass down and said: "Thank you for whatever it was. Now let's talk."

"Gladly, gladly!" boomed Mr. Roosenburg. "Kathryn, the files!"

Garrick looked after her, shaking his head. Not only was she a statistician, which was robot work, she was also a file clerk—and that was barely even robot work, it was the kind of thing handled by a semisentient punch-card sorter in a decently run sector.

Roosenburg said sharply: "Shocks you, doesn't it? But that's why you're here." He was a slim, fair little man, and he wore a golden beard cropped square.

Garrick took another sip of the fizzy drink. It was good stuff; it didn't intoxicate, but it cheered. He said, "I'm glad to know why I'm here."

The golden beard quivered. "Area Control sent you down and didn't tell you this was a disaster area?"

Garrick put down the glass. "I'm a psychist. Area Control said you needed a psychist. From what I've seen, it's a supply problem, but——"

"Here are the files," said Kathryn Pender, and stood watching him.

Roosenburg took the spools of tape from her and dropped them in his lap. He said tangentially, "How old are you, Roger?"

Garrick was annoyed. "I'm a qualified psychist! I happen to be assigned to Area Control and——"

"How old are you?"

Garrick scowled. "Twenty-four."

Roosenburg nodded. "Um. Rather young," he observed. "Maybe you don't remember how things used to be."

Garrick said dangerously, "All the information I need is on that tape. I don't need any lectures from you."

Roosenburg pursed his lips and got up. "Come here a minute, will you?"

He moved over to the rail of the sun deck and pointed. "See those things down there?"

Garrick looked. Twenty stories down the village straggled off toward the sea in a tangle of pastel oblongs and towers. Over the bay the hills of the mainland were faintly visible through mist; and riding the bay, the flat white floats of the solar receptors.

"It's a power plant. That what you mean?"

Roosenburg boomed, "A power plant. All the power the world can ever use, out of this one and all the others, all over the world." He peered out at the bobbing floats, soaking up energy from the sun. "And people used to try to wreck them," he said.

Garrick said stiffly: "I may only be twenty-four years old, Mr. Roosenburg, but I have completed school."

"Oh, yes. Oh, of course you have, Roger. But maybe schooling isn't the same thing as living through a time like that. I grew up in the Era of Plenty, when the law was: *Consume*. My parents were poor, and I still remember the misery of my childhood. Eat and consume, wear and use. I never had a moment's peace, Roger! For the very poor it was a treadmill; we had to consume so much that we could never catch up, and the farther we fell behind, the more the Ration Board forced on us——"

Roger Garrick said: "That's ancient history, Mr. Roosenburg. Morey Fry liberated us from all that."

The girl said softly: "Not all of us."

The man with the golden beard nodded. "Not all of us. As you should know, Roger, being a psychist."

Garrick sat up straight, and Roosenburg went on: "Fry showed us that the robots could help at both ends—by making, by consuming. But it came a little late for some of us. The patterns of childhood—they linger on."

Kathryn Pender leaned toward Garrick. "What he's trying to say, Mr. Garrick—we've got a compulsive consumer on our hands."

III

North Guardian Island—nine miles away. It wasn't as much as a mile wide, and not much more than that in length. But it had its city and its bathing beaches, its parks and theaters. It was possibly the most densely populated island in the world . . . for the number of its inhabitants.

The President of the Council convened their afternoon meeting in a large and lavish room. There were nineteen councilmen around a lustrous mahogany table. Over the President's shoulder the others could see the situation map of North Guardian and the areas surrounding. North Guardian glowed blue, cool, impregnable. The sea was misty green; the mainland, Fisherman's Island, South Guardian and the rest of the little archipelago were a hot and hostile red.

Little flickering fingers of red attacked the blue. Flick, and a ruddy flame wiped out a corner of a beach; flick, and a red spark appeared in the middle of the city, to grow and blossom, and then to die. Each little red whip-flick was a point where, momentarily, the defenses of the island were down; but always and always, the cool blue brightened around the red, and drowned it.

The President was tall, stooped, old. It wore glasses,

though robot eyes saw well enough without. It said, in a voice that throbbed with power and pride: "The first item of the order of business will be a report of the Defense Secretary."

The Defense Secretary rose to its feet, hooked a thumb in its vest and cleared its throat. "Mr. President——"

"Excuse me, sir." A whisper from the sweet-faced young blonde taking down the minutes of the meeting. "Mr. Trumie has just left Bowling Green, heading north."

The whole council turned to glance at the situation map, where Bowling Green had just flared red.

The President nodded stiffly, like the crown of an old redwood nodding. "You may proceed, Mr. Secretary," it said after a moment.

"Our invasion fleet," began the Secretary, in its high, clear voice, "is ready for sailing on the first suitable tide. Certain units have been, ah, inactivated, at the, ah, instigation of Mr. Trumie, but on the whole repairs have been completed and the units will be serviceable within the next few hours." Its lean, attractive face turned solemn. "I am afraid, however, that the Air Command has sustained certain, ah, increments of attrition—due, I should emphasize, to chances involved in certain calculated risks——"

"Question, question!" It was the Commissioner of Public Safety, small, dark, fire-eyed, angry.

"Mr. Commissioner?" the President began, but it was interrupted again by the soft whisper of the recording stenographer, listening intently to the earphones that brought news from outside.

"Mr. President," it whispered, "Mr. Trumie has passed the Navy Yard." The robots turned to look at the situation map. Bowling Green, though it smoldered in spots, had mostly gone back to blue. But the jagged oblong of the Yard flared red and bright. There was a faint electronic hum in the air, almost a sigh.

The robots turned back to face each other. "Mr. President! I demand the Defense Secretary explain the loss of the *Graf Zeppelin* and the 456th Bomb Group!"

The Defense Secretary nodded to the Commissioner of Public Safety. "Mr. Trumie threw them away," it said sorrowfully.

Once again, that sighing electronic drone from the assembled robots.

The Council fussed and fiddled with its papers, while the situation map on the wall flared and dwindled, flared and dwindled. The Defense Secretary cleared its throat again. "Mr. President, there is no question that the, ah, absence of an effective air component will seriously hamper, not to say endanger, our prospects of a suitable landing. Nevertheless—and I say this, Mr. President, in full knowledge of the conclusions that may —indeed, should!—be drawn from such a statement— nevertheless, Mr. President, I say that our forward elements will successfully complete an assault landing——"

"Mr. President!" The breathless whisper of the blonde stenographer again. "Mr. President, Mr. Trumie is in the building!"

On the situation map behind it, the Pentagon—the building they were in—flared scarlet.

The Attorney General, nearest the door, leaped to its feet. "Mr. President, I hear him!"

And they could all hear, now. Far off, down the long corridors, a crash. A faint explosion, and another crash; and a raging, querulous, high-pitched voice. A nearer crash, and a sustained, smashing, banging sound, coming toward them.

The oak-paneled doors flew open, splintering.

A tall, dark male figure in gray leather jacket, rocket-gun holsters swinging at its hips, stepped through the splintered doors and stood surveying the Council. Its hands hung just below the butts of the rocket guns.

It drawled: "Mistuh Anderson Trumie!"

It stepped aside. Another male figure—shorter, darker, hobbling with the aid of a stainless steel cane that concealed a ray-pencil, wearing the same gray leather jacket and the same rocket-gun holsters—entered, stood for a moment, and took a position on the other side of the door.

Between them, Mr. Anderson Trumie shambled ponderously into the Council Chamber to call on his Council.

Sonny Trumie, come of age.

He wasn't much more than five feet tall; but his weight

was close to four hundred pounds. He stood there in
the door, leaning against the splintered oak, quivering
jowls obliterating his neck, his eyes nearly swallowed in
the fat that swamped his skull, his thick legs trembling
as they tried to support him.

"You're all under arrest!" he shrilled. "Traitors! Traitors!"

He panted ferociously, staring at them. They waited
with bowed heads. Beyond the ring of councilmen, the
situation map slowly blotted out the patches of red, as
the repair-robots worked feverishly to fix what Sonny
Trumie had destroyed.

"Mr. Crockett!" he cried shrilly. "Slay me these traitors!"

Wheep-wheep, and the guns whistled out of their holsters into the tall bodyguard's hands. *Rata-tat-tat,* and
two by two, the nineteen councilmen leaped, clutched
at air and fell, as the rocket pellets pierced them through.

"That one too!" cried Mr. Trumie, pointing at the
sweet-faced blonde. *Bang.* The sweet young face con-
vulsed and froze; it fell, slumping across its little table.
On the wall the situation map flared red again, but
only faintly—for what were twenty robots?

Sonny gestured curtly to his other bodyguard. It
leaped forward, tucking the stainless-steel cane under
one arm, putting the other around the larded shoulders
of Sonny Trumie. "Ah, now, young master," it crooned.
"You just get ahold o' Long John's arm now——"

"Get them fixed," Sonny ordered abruptly. He pushed
the President of the Council out of its chair and, with the
robot's help, sank into it himself. "Get them fixed *right,*
you hear? I've had enough traitors. I want them to do
what I tell them!"

"Sartin sure, young marster. Long John'll——"

"Do it *now!* And you, Davey! I want my lunch."

"Reckoned you would, Mistuh Trumie. It's right hyar."
The Crockett-robot kicked the fallen councilmen out
of the way as a procession of waiters filed in from the
corridor.

He ate.

He ate until eating was pain, and then he sat there
sobbing, his arms braced against the tabletop, until he

could eat more. The Crockett-robot said worriedly: "Mistuh Trumie, moughtn't you hold back a little? Old Doc Aeschylus, he don't keer much to have you eatin' too much, you know."

"I hate Doc!" Trumie said bitterly. He pushed the plates off the table. They fell with a rattle and a clatter, and they went spinning away as he heaved himself up and lurched alone over to the window. "I hate Doc!" he brayed again, sobbing, staring through tears out the window at his kingdom with its hurrying throngs and marching troops and roaring waterfront. The tallow shoulders tried to shake with pain. He felt as though hot cinderblocks were being thrust up into his body cavities, the ragged edges cutting, the hot weight crushing. "Take me back," he sobbed to the robots. "Take me away from these traitors. Take me to my Private Place!"

IV

"So you see," said Roosenburg, "he's dangerous."

Garrick looked out over the water, toward North Guardian. "I'd better look at his tapes," he said. The girl swiftly picked up the reels and began to thread them into the projector. Dangerous. This Trumie was dangerous, all right, Garrick conceded. Dangerous to the balanced, stable world; for it only took one Trumie to topple its stability. It had taken thousands and thousands of years for society to learn its delicate tightrope walk. It was a matter for a psychist, all right. . . .

And Garrick was uncomfortably aware that he was only twenty-four.

"Here you are," said the girl.

"Look them over," said Roosenburg. "Then, after you've studied the tapes on Trumie, we've got something else. One of his robots. But you'll need the tapes first."

"Let's go," said Garrick.

The girl flicked a switch, and the life of Anderson Trumie appeared before them, in color, in three dimensions—in miniature.

Robots have eyes; and where the robots go, the eyes of Robot Central go with them. And the robots go everywhere. From the stored files of Robot Central came the spool of tape that was the life story of Sonny Trumie.

The tapes played into the globe-shaped viewer, ten inches high, a crystal ball that looked back into the past. First, from the recording eyes of the robots in Sonny Trumie's nursery. The lonely little boy, twenty years before, lost in the enormous nursery.

"Disgusting!" breathed Kathryn Pender, wrinkling her nose. "How could people live like that?"

Garrick said, "Please, let me watch this. It's important." In the gleaming globe the little boy-figure kicked at his toys, threw himself across his huge bed, sobbed. Garrick squinted, frowned, reached out, tried to make contact. . . . It was hard. The tapes showed the objective facts, all right; but for a psychist it was the subjective reality behind the facts that mattered. Kicking at his toys. Yes, but why? Because he was tired of them—and why was he tired? Because he feared them? *Kicking at his toys.* Because—because they were the *wrong* toys? *Kicking— hate them! Don't want them! Want—*

A bluish flare in the viewing globe. Garrick blinked and jumped; and that was the end of that section.

The colors flowed, and suddenly jelled into bright life. Anderson Trumie, a young man. Garrick recognized the scene after a moment—it was right there on Fisherman's Island, some pleasure spot overlooking the water. A bar, and at the end of it was Anderson Trumie, pimply and twenty, staring somberly into an empty glass. The view was through the eyes of the robot bartender.

Anderson Trumie was weeping.

Once again, there was the objective fact—but the fact behind the fact, what was it? Trumie had been drinking, drinking. Why? *Drinking, drinking.* With a sudden sense of shock, Garrick saw what the drink was—the golden, fizzy liquor. Not intoxicating. Not habit-forming! Trumie had become no drunk, it was something else that kept him *drinking, drinking, must drink, must keep on drinking, or else—*

And again the bluish flare.

There was more; there was Trumie feverishly collecting objects of art, there was Trumie decorating a palace;

there was Trumie on a world tour, and Trumie returned to Fisherman's Island.

And then there was no more.

"That," said Roosenburg, "is the file. Of course, if you want the raw, unedited tapes, we can try to get them from Robot Central, but——"

"No." The way things were, it was best to stay away from Robot Central; there might be more breakdowns, and there wasn't much time. Besides, something was beginning to suggest itself.

"Run the first one again," said Garrick. "I think maybe there's something there...."

Garrick made out a quick requisition slip and handed it to Kathryn Pender, who looked at it, raised her eyebrows, shrugged and went off to have it filled.

By the time she came back, Roosenburg had escorted Garrick to the room where the captured Trumie robot lay enchained. "He's cut off from Robot Central," Roosenburg was saying. "I suppose you figured that out. Imagine! Not only has he built a whole city for himself—but even his own robot control!"

Garrick looked at the robot. It was a fisherman, or so Roosenburg had said. It was small, dark, black-haired, and possibly the hair would have been curly, if the sea water hadn't plastered the curls to the scalp. It was still damp from the tussle that had landed it in the water, and eventually in Roosenburg's hands.

Roosenburg was already at work. Garrick tried to think of it as a machine, but it wasn't easy. The thing looked very nearly human—except for the crystal and copper that showed where the back of its head had been removed.

"It's as bad as a brain operation," said Roosenburg, working rapidly without looking up. "I've got to short out the input leads without disturbing the electronic balance...."

Snip, snip. A curl of copper fell free, to be grabbed by Roosenburg's tweezers. The fisherman's arms and legs kicked sharply like a galvanized frog's.

Kathryn Pender said: "They found him this morning,

casting nets into the bay and singing *O Sole Mio*. He's from North Guardian, all right."

Abruptly the lights flickered and turned yellow, then slowly returned to normal brightness. Roger Garrick got up and walked over to the window. North Guardian was a haze of light in the sky, across the water.

Click, snap. The fisherman-robot began to sing:

> *Tutte le serre, dopo quel fanal,*
> *Dietro la caserma, ti starò ed—*

Click. Roosenburg muttered under his breath and probed further. Kathryn Pender joined Garrick at the window. "Now you see," she said.

Garrick shrugged. "You can't blame him."

"*I* blame him!" she said hotly. "I've lived here all my life. Fisherman's Island used to be a tourist spot—why, it was lovely here. And look at it now. The elevators don't work. The lights don't work. Practically all of our robots are gone. Spare parts, construction material, everything —it's all gone to North Guardian! There isn't a day that passes, Garrick, when half a dozen bargeloads of stuff don't go north, because *he* requisitioned them. Blame him? I'd like to kill him!"

Snap. Sputter*snap*. The fisherman lifted its head and caroled:

> *Forse dommani, piangerai,*
> *E dopo tu, sorriderai—*

Snap. Roosenburg's probe uncovered a flat black disc. "Kathryn, look this up, will you?" He read the serial number from the disc, and then put down the probe. He stood flexing his fingers, staring irritably at the motionless figure.

Garrick joined him. Roosenburg jerked his head at the fisherman. "That's robot work, trying to tinker with their insides. Trumie has his own control center, you see. What I have to do is recontrol this one from the substation on the mainland, but keep its receptor circuits open to North Guardian on the symbolic level. You understand

what I'm talking about? It'll think from North Guardian,
but act from the mainland."

"Sure," said Garrick, far from sure.

"And it's damned close work. There isn't much room
inside one of those things. . . ." He stared at the figure
and picked up the probe again.

Kathryn Pender came back with a punchcard in her
hand. "It was one of ours, all right. Used to be a busboy
in the cafeteria at the beach club." She scowled. "That
Trumie!"

"You can't blame him," Garrick said reasonably. "He's
only trying to be good."

She looked at him queerly. "He's only—" she began;
but Roosenburg interrupted with an exultant cry.

"Got it! All right, you. Sit up and start telling us what
Trumie's up to now!"

The fisherman figure said obligingly, "Sure, boss.
Whatcha wanna know?"

What they wanted to know they asked; and what they
asked it told them, volunteering nothing, concealing
nothing.

There was Anderson Trumie, king of his island, the
compulsive consumer.

It was like an echo of the bad old days of the Age of
Plenty, when the world was smothering under the endless, pounding flow of goods from the robot factories
and the desperate race between consumption and production strained the human fabric. But Trumie's orders
came not from society, but from within. *Consume!* commanded something inside him, and *Use!* it cried, and
Devour! it ordered. And Trumie obeyed, heroically.

They listened to what the fisherman-robot had to say,
and the picture was dark. Armies had sprung up on
North Guardian, navies floated in its waters. Anderson
Trumie stalked among his creations like a blubbery god,
wrecking and ruling. Garrick could see the pattern in
what the fisherman had to say. In Trumie's mind, he
was Hitler, Hoover and Genghis Khan; he was dictator,
building a war machine; he was supreme engineer, con-
structing a mighty state. He was warrior.

"He was playing tin soldiers," said Roger Garrick, and Roosenburg and the girl nodded.

"The trouble is," boomed Roosenburg, "he has stopped playing. Invasion fleets, Garrick! He isn't content with North Guardian any more, he wants the rest of the country too!"

"You can't blame him," said Roger Garrick for the third time, and stood up.

"The question is," he said, "what do we do about it?"

"That's what you're here for," Kathryn told him.

"All right. We can forget," said Roger Garrick, "about the soldiers—*qua* soldiers, that is. I promise you they won't hurt anyone. Robots can't."

"I understand that," Kathryn snapped.

"The problem is what to do about Trumie's drain on the world's resources." He pursed his lips. "According to my directive from Area Control, the first plan was to let him alone—after all, there is still plenty of everything for anyone. Why not let Trumie enjoy himself? But that didn't work out too well."

"You are so right," said Kathryn Pender.

"No, no—not on your local level," Garrick explained quickly. "After all—what are a few thousand robots, a few hundred million dollars worth of equipment? We could resupply this area in a week."

"And in a week," boomed Roosenburg, "Trumie would have us cleaned out again!"

Garrick nodded. "That's the trouble," he admitted. "He doesn't seem to have a stopping point. Yet—we can't *refuse* his orders. Speaking as a psychist, that would set a very bad precedent. It would put ideas in the minds of a lot of persons—minds that, in some cases, might not be reliably stable in the absence of a stable, certain source of everything they need, on request. If we say 'no' to Trumie, we open the door on some mighty dark corners of the human mind. Covetousness. Greed. Pride of possession——"

"So what are you going to do?" cried Kathryn Pender.

Garrick said resentfully, "The only thing there is *to* do. I'm going to look over Trumie's folder again. And then I'm going to North Guardian Island."

V

Roger Garrick was all too aware of the fact that he was only twenty-four.

It didn't make a great deal of difference. The oldest and wisest psychist in Area Control's wide sphere might have been doubtful of success in as thorny a job as the one ahead.

They started out at daybreak. Vapor was rising from the sea about them, and the little battery motor of their launch whined softly beneath the keelson. Garrick sat patting the little box that contained their invasion equipment, while the girl steered. The workshops of Fisherman's Island had been all night making some of the things in that box—not because they were so difficult to make, but because it had been a bad night. Big things were going on at North Guardian; twice the power had been out entirely for nearly an hour, as the demand on the lines from North Guardian took all the power the system could deliver.

The sun was well up as they came within hailing distance of the Navy Yard.

Robots were hard at work; the Yard was bustling with activity. An overhead traveling crane, eight feet tall, laboriously lowered a prefabricated fighting top onto an eleven-foot aircraft carrier. A motor torpedo boat—full-sized, this one was, not to scale—rocked at anchor just before the bow of their launch. Kathryn steered around it, ignoring the hail from the robot-lieutenant-j.g. at its rail.

She glanced at Garrick over her shoulder, her face taut. "It's—it's all mixed up."

Garrick nodded. The battleships were model-sized, the small boats full scale. In the city beyond the Yard, the pinnacle of the Empire State Building barely cleared the Pentagon, next door. A soaring suspension bridge leaped out from the shore a quarter of a mile away, and stopped short a thousand yards out, over empty water.

It was easy enough to understand—even for a psychist just out of school, on his first real assignment. Trumie was trying to run a world singlehanded, and where there were gaps in his conception of what his world should be, the results showed. "Get me battleships!" he ordered his robot supply clerks; and they found the only battleships there were in the world to copy, the child-sized, toy-scaled play battleships that still delighted kids. "Get me an Air Force!" And a thousand model bombers were hastily put together. "Build me a bridge!" But perhaps he had forgot to say to where.

"Come on, Garrick!"

He shook his head and focused on the world around him. Kathryn Pender was standing on a gray steel stage, the mooring line from their launch secured to what looked like a coast-defense cannon—but only about four feet long. Garrick picked up his little box and leaped up to the stage beside her. She turned to look at the city. . . .

"Hold on a second." He was opening the box, taking out two little cardboard placards. He turned her by the shoulder and, with pins from the box, attached one of the cards to her back. "Now me," he said, turning his back to her.

She read the placard dubiously:

I
AM A
SPY!

"Garrick," she began, "you're sure you know what you're doing——"

"Put it on!" She shrugged and pinned it to the folds of his jacket.

Side by side, they entered the citadel of the enemy.

According to the fisherman-robot, Trumie lived in a gingerbread castle south of the Pentagon. Most of the robots got no chance to enter it. The city outside the castle was Trumie's kingdom, and he roamed about it, overseeing, changing, destroying, rebuilding. But inside the castle was his Private Place; the only robots that had both an inside- and outside-the-castle existence were his two bodyguards.

"That," said Garrick, "must be the Private Place."

It was a gingerbread castle, all right. The "gingerbread" was stonework, gargoyles and columns; there was a moat and a drawbridge, and there were robot guards with crooked little rifles, wearing scarlet tunics and fur shakos three feet tall. The drawbridge was up and the guards at stiff attention.

"Let's reconnoiter," said Garrick. He was unpleasantly conscious of the fact that every robot they passed—and they had passed thousands—had turned to look at the signs on their backs. Yet—it was right, wasn't it? There was no hope of avoiding observation in any event. The only hope was to fit somehow into the pattern—and spies would certainly be a part of the pattern. Wouldn't they?

Garrick turned his back on doubts and led the way around the gingerbread palace.

The only entrance was the drawbridge.

They stopped out of sight of the ramrod-stiff guards. Garrick said: "We'll go in. As soon as we get inside, you put on your costume." He handed her the box. "You know what to do. All you have to do is keep him quiet for a while and let me talk to him."

The girl said doubtfully, "Garrick. Is this going to work?"

Garrick exploded: "How the devil do I know? I had Trumie's dossier to work with. I know everything that happened to him when he was a kid—when this trouble started. But to reach him, to talk to the boy inside the man—that takes a long time, Kathryn. And we don't have a long time. So. . . ."

He took her elbow and marched her toward the guards. "So you know what to do," he said.

"I hope so," breathed Kathryn Pender, looking very small and very young.

They marched down the wide white pavement, past the motionless guards. . . .

Something was coming toward them. Kathryn held back. "Come on!" Garrick muttered.

"No, look!" she whispered. "Is that—is that Trumie?"

He looked.

It was Trumie, larger than life. It was Anderson Trumie, the entire human population of the most-congested-island-for-its-population in the world. On one side of

him was a tall dark figure, on the other side a squat dark
figure, helping him along. They looked at his face and
it was horror, drowned in fat. The bloated cheeks shook
damply, wet with tears. The eyes looked out with fright
on the world he had made.

Trumie and his bodyguards rolled up to them and
past. And then Anderson Trumie stopped.

He turned the blubbery head, and read the sign on the
back of the girl. *I am a spy*. Panting heavily, clutching
the shoulder of the Crockett-robot, he stared wildly at
her.

Garrick cleared his throat. This far his plan had gone,
and then there was a gap. There had to be a gap. Trumie's history, in the folder that Roosenburg had supplied,
had told him what to do with Trumie; and Garrick's
own ingenuity had told him how to reach the man. But a
link was missing. Here was the subject, and here was the
psychist who could cure him; and it was up to Garrick
to start the cure.

Trumie cried, in a staccato bleat: "You! What are you?
Where do you belong?"

He was talking to the girl. Beside him the Crockett-
robot murmured, "Rackin she's a spy, Mistuh Trumie.
See thet sign a-hangin' on her back?"

"Spy? Spy?" The quivering lips pouted. "Curse you,
are you Mata Hari? What are you doing out here? It's
changed its face," Trumie complained to the Crockett-
robot. "It doesn't belong here. It's supposed to be in the
harem. Go on, Crockett, get it back!"

"Wait!" cried Garrick, but the Crockett-robot was
ahead of him. It took Kathryn Pender by the arm.

"Come along thar," it said soothingly, and urged her
across the drawbridge. She glanced back at Garrick, and
for a moment it looked as though she were going to
speak. Then she shook her head, as though she were giving an order.

"Kathryn!" cried Garrick. "Trumie, wait a minute.
That isn't Mata Hari!"

No one was listening. Kathryn Pender disappeared
into the Private Place. Trumie, leaning heavily on the
hobbling Silver-robot, followed.

Garrick, coming back to life, leaped after them. . . .

The scarlet-coated guards jumped before him, their shakos bobbing, their crooked little rifles crossed to bar his way.

He cried, "One side! Out of my way, you! I'm a human, don't you understand? You've got to let me pass!"

They didn't even look at him; trying to get by them was like trying to walk through a wall of moving, thrusting steel. He shoved, and they pushed him back; he tried to dodge, and they were before him. It was hopeless.

And then it was hopeless indeed, because behind them, he saw, the drawbridge had gone up.

VI

Sonny Trumie collapsed into a chair like a mound of blubber falling to the deck of a whaler.

Though he made no signal, the procession of serving robots started at once. In minced the maître d', bowing and waving its graceful hands; in marched the sommelier, clanking its necklace of keys, bearing its wines in their buckets of ice. In came the lovely waitress-robots and the sturdy steward-robots, with the platters and tureens, the plates and bowls and cups. They spread a meal—a dozen meals—before him, and he began to eat. He ate as a penned pig eats, gobbling until it chokes, forcing the food down because there is nothing to do *but* eat. He ate, with a sighing accompaniment of moans and gasps, and some of the food was salted with the tears of pain he wept into it, and some of the wine was spilled by his shaking hand. But he ate. Not for the first time that day, and not for the tenth.

Sonny Trumie wept as he ate. He no longer even knew he was weeping. There was the gaping void inside him that he had to fill, had to fill; there was the gaping world about him that he had to people and build and furnish—and *use*. He moaned to himself. Four hundred pounds of meat and lard, and he had to lug it from end to end of his island, every hour of every day, never resting, never at peace! There should have been a place somewhere, there should have been a time, when he could rest. When he could sleep without dreaming, sleep without waking after a scant few hours with the goading drive to eat and to use, to use and to eat. . . . And it was all so *wrong!* The robots didn't understand. They didn't try to understand, they didn't think for themselves. Let him take his eyes from any one of them for a single day, and everything went *wrong.* It was necessary to keep after them, from end to end of the island, checking and overseeing and ordering—yes, and destroying to rebuild, over and over!

He moaned again, and pushed the plate away.

He rested, with his tallow forehead flat against the table, waiting, while inside him the pain ripped and ripped, and finally became bearable again. And slowly he pushed himself up again, and rested for a moment, and pulled a fresh plate toward him, and began again to eat. . . .

After a while he stopped. Not because he didn't want to go on, but because he couldn't.

He was bone-tired, but something was bothering him— one more detail to check, one more thing that was *wrong.* The houri at the drawbridge. It shouldn't have been out of the Private Place. It should have been in the harem, of course. Not that it mattered, except to Sonny Trumie's sense of what was right. Time was when the houris of the harem had their uses, but that time was long and long ago; now they were property, to be fussed over and made to be *right,* to be replaced if they were worn, destroyed if they were *wrong.* But only property, as all of North Guardian was property—as all of the world would be his property, if only he could manage it.

But property shouldn't be *wrong.*

He signaled to the Crockett-robot and, leaning on it, walked down the long terrazzo hall toward the harem. He tried to remember what the houri had looked like. It had worn a sheer red blouse and a brief red skirt, he was nearly sure, but the face. . . . It had had a face, of course. But Sonny had lost the habit of faces. This one had been somehow different, but he couldn't remember just why. Still—the blouse and skirt, they were red, he was nearly sure. And it had been carrying something in a box. And that was odd, too.

He waddled a little faster, for now he was sure it was *wrong.*

"That's the harem, Mistuh Trumie," said the robot at his side. It disengaged itself gently, leaped forward and held the door to the harem for him.

"Wait for me," Sonny commanded, and waddled forward into the harem halls. Once he had so arranged the harem that he needed no help inside it; the halls were railed, at a height where it was easy for a pudgy hand to grasp the rail; the distances were short, the rooms close together. He paused and called over his shoulder, "Stay where you can hear me." It had occurred to him that if the houri-robot was *wrong*, he would need Crockett's guns to make it right.

A chorus of female voices sprang into song as he entered the main patio. They were a bevy of beauties, clustered around a fountain, diaphanously dressed, languorously glancing at Sonny Trumie as he waddled inside. "Shut up!" he commanded. "Go back to your rooms." They bowed their heads and, one by one, slipped into the cubicles.

No sign of the red blouse and the red skirt. He began the rounds of the cubicles, panting, peering into them. "Hello, Sonny," whispered Theda Bara, lithe on a leopard rug, and he passed on. "I love you!" cried Nell Gwynn, and, "Come to me!" commanded Cleopatra, but he passed them by. He passed Dubarry and Marilyn Monroe, he passed Moll Flanders and he passed Troy's Helen. No sign of the houri in red. . . .

And then he saw signs. He didn't see the houri, but he saw the signs of the houri's presence; the red blouse and the red skirt, lying limp and empty on the floor.

Sonny gasped, "You! Where are you? Come out here where I can see you!"

Nobody answered Sonny. "Come out!" he bawled.

· And then he stopped. A door opened and someone came out; not a houri, not female; a figure without sex but loaded with love, a teddy-bear figure, as tall as pudgy Sonny Trumie himself, waddling as he waddled, its stubbed arms stretched out to him.

Sonny could hardly believe his eyes. Its color was a little darker than Teddy. It was a good deal taller than Teddy. But unquestionably, undoubtedly, in everything that mattered it was—"Teddy," whispered Sonny Trumie, and let the furry arms go around his four hundred pounds.

Twenty years disappeared. "They wouldn't let me have you," Sonny told the teddy; and it said, in a voice musical and warm:
"It's all right, Sonny. You can have me now, Sonny. You can have everything, Sonny."
"They took you away," he whispered, remembering. They took the teddy-bear away; he had never forgotten. They took it away, and they were wild. Mother was wild, and father was furious; they raged at the little boy and scolded him, and threatened him. Didn't he know they were *poor*, and did he want to ruin them all, and what was wrong with him anyway, that he wanted his little sister's silly stuffed robots when he was big enough to use nearly grown-up goods.
The night had been a terror, with the frowning, sad robots ringed around and the little girl crying; and what had made it terror was not the scolding—he'd had scoldings—but the *worry*, the fear and almost the panic in his parents' voices. For what he did, he came to understand, was no longer a childish sin; it was a *big* sin, a failure to consume his quota—
And it had to be punished. The first punishment was the extra birthday party; the second was—shame. Sonny Trumie, not quite twelve, was made to feel shame and humiliation. Shame is only a little thing, but it makes the one who owns it little too. Shame. The robots were reset to scorn him. He woke to mockery, and went to bed with contempt. Even his little sister lisped the catalogue of his failures. You aren't trying, Sonny, and You don't care, Sonny, and You're a terrible disappointment to us, Sonny. And finally all the things were true; because Sonny at twelve was what his elders made him.
And they made him . . . "neurotic" is the term; a pretty-sounding word that means ugly things like fear and worry and endless self-reproach. . . .
"Don't worry," whispered the teddy. "Don't worry, Sonny. You can have me. You can have what you want. You don't have to have anything else. . . ."

VII

Garrick raged through the halls of the Private Place like a tiger upon a kid. "Kathryn!" he cried. "Kathryn Pender!" Finally he had found a way in, unguarded, forgotten. But it had taken time. And he was worried. "Kathryn!" The robots peeped out at him, worriedly, and sometimes they got in his way and he bowled them aside. They didn't fight back, naturally—what robot would hurt a human? But sometimes they spoke to him, pleading, for it was not according to the wishes of Mr. Trumie that anyone but him rage destroying through North Guardian Island. He passed them by. "Kathryn!" he called. "Kathryn!"

It wasn't that Trumie was dangerous.

He told himself fiercely: Trumie was *not* dangerous. Trumie was laid bare in his folder, the one that Roosenburg had supplied. He couldn't be blamed, and he meant no harm. He was once a bad little boy who was trying to be good by consuming, consuming; and he wore himself into neurosis doing it; and then they changed the rules on him. End of the ration; end of forced consumption, as the robots took over for mankind at the other end of the cornucopia. It wasn't necessary to struggle to consume, so the rules were changed. . . .

And maybe Mr. Trumie knew that the rules had been changed; but Sonny didn't. It was Sonny, the bad little boy trying to be good, who had made North Guardian Island. . . .

And it was Sonny who owned the Private Place, and all it held—including Kathryn Pender.

Garrick called hoarsely, "Kathryn! If you hear me, *answer me!*"

It had seemed so simple. The fulcrum on which the weight of Trumie's neurosis might move was a teddy-bear; give him a teddy-bear—or, perhaps, a teddy-bear suit, made by night in the factories of Fisherman's Island, with a girl named Kathryn Pender inside—and let him hear, from a source he could trust, the welcome news that it was no longer necessary to struggle, that compulsive consumption could have an end. Permissive analysis would clear it up; but only if Trumie would listen.

"Kathryn!" roared Roger Garrick, racing through a room of mirrors and carved statues. Because, just in case Trumie didn't listen, just in case the folder was wrong and the teddy wasn't the key—

Why, then, the teddy to Trumie was only a robot. And Trumie destroyed them by the score.

"Kathryn!" cried Roger Garrick, trotting through the silent palace; and at last he heard what might have been an answer. At least it was a voice—a girl's voice, at that. He was before a passage that led to a room with a fountain and silent female robots, standing and watching him. The voice came from a small room. He ran to the door.

It was the right door.

There was Trumie, four hundred pounds of lard, lying on a marble bench with a foam-rubber cushion, the jowled head in the small lap of—

Teddy. Or Kathryn Pender in the teddy-bear suit, the stick-like legs pointed straight out, the stick-like arms clumsily patting him. She was talking to him, gently and reassuringly. She was telling him what he needed to know—that he had eaten *enough*, that he had used *enough*, that he had consumed enough to win the respect of all, and an end to consuming.

Garrick himself could not have done better.

It was a sight from Mother Goose, the child being soothed by his toy. But it was not a sight that fit in well with its surroundings, for the seraglio was upholstered in mauve and pink, and wicked paintings hung about.

Sonny Trumie rolled the pendulous head and looked squarely at Garrick. The worry was gone from the fearful little eyes.

Garrick stepped back.

No need for him just at this moment. Let Trumie relax for a while, as he had not been able to relax for a score of years. Then the psychist could pick up where the girl had been unable to proceed; but in the meantime, Trumie was finally at rest.

The teddy looked up at Garrick, and in its bright blue eyes, the eyes that belonged to the girl named Kathryn, he saw a queer tincture of triumph and compassion.

Garrick nodded and left, and went out to the robots of North Guardian and started them clearing away.

Sonny Trumie nestled his swine's head in the lap of the teddy-bear. It was talking to him so nicely, so nicely. It was droning away, "Don't worry, Sonny. Don't worry. Everything's all right. Everything's all right." Why, it was almost as though it were real.

It had been, he calculated with the part of his mind that was razor-sharp and never relaxed, it had been nearly two hours since he had eaten. Two hours! And he felt as though he could go another hour at least, maybe two. Maybe—maybe even not eat at all again that day. Maybe even learn to live on three meals. Perhaps two. Perhaps—

He wriggled—as well as four hundred greasy pounds can wriggle—and pressed against the soft warm fur of the teddy-bear. It was so soothing! "You don't have to eat so much, Sonny. You don't have to drink so much. No one will mind. Your father won't mind, Sonny. Your mother won't mind. . . ."

It was very comfortable to hear the teddy-bear telling him those things. It made him drowsy. So deliciously drowsy! It wasn't like going to sleep, as Sonny Trumie had known going to sleep for a dozen or more years, the bitterly fought surrender to the anesthetic weariness. It was just drowsy. . . ..

And he did want to go to sleep.

And finally he slept. All of him slept. Not just the four hundred pounds of blubber and the little pig eyes, but even the razor-sharp mind-Trumie that lived in the sad, obedient hulk; it slept; and it had never slept before.

THE WIZARDS OF PUNG'S CORNERS

I

THIS is the way it happened in the old days. Pay attention now. I'm not going to repeat myself.

There was this old man. A wicked one. Coglan was his name, and he came into Pung's Corners in a solid-lead car. He was six feet seven inches tall. He attracted a lot of attention.

Why? Why, because nobody had ever seen a solid-lead car before. Nobody much had ever seen a stranger. It wasn't usual. That was how Pung's Corners was in the old days, a little pocket in the middle of the desert, and nobody came there. There weren't even planes overhead, or not for a long time; but there had been planes just before old man Coglan showed up. It made people nervous.

Old man Coglan had snapping black eyes and a loose and limber step. He got out of his car and slammed the door closed. It didn't go *tchik* like a Volkswagen or *perclack* like a Buick. It went *woomp*. It was heavy, since, as I mentioned, it was solid lead.

"Boy!" he bellowed, standing in front of Pung's Inn. "Come get my bags!"

Charley Frink was the bellboy at that time—yes, the Senator. Of course, he was only fifteen years old then. He came out for Coglan's bags and he had to make four trips. There was a lot of space in the back of that car, with its truck tires and double-thick glass, and all of it was full of baggage.

While Charley was hustling the bags in, Coglan was parading back and forth on Front Street. He winked at Mrs. Churchwood and ogled young Kathy

38

Flint. He nodded to the boys in front of the barber shop. He was a character, making himself at home like that.

In front of Andy Grammis's grocery store, Andy tipped his chair back. Considerately, he moved his feet so his yellow dog could get out the door. "He seems like a nice feller," he said to Jack Tighe. (Yes, *that* Jack Tighe.)

Jack Tighe stood in the shelter of the door and he was frowning. He knew more than any of the rest of them, though it wasn't time to say anything yet. But he said: "We don't get any strangers."

Andy shrugged. He leaned back in his chair. It was warm in the sun.

"Pshaw, Jack," he said. "Maybe we ought to get a few more. Town's going to sleep." He yawned drowsily.

And Jack Tighe left him there, left him and started down the street for home, because he knew what he knew.

Anyway, Coglan didn't hear them. If he had heard, he wouldn't have cared. It was old man Coglan's great talent that he didn't care what people had to say about him, and the others like him. He couldn't have been what he was if that hadn't been so.

So he checked in at Pung's Inn. "A suite, boy!" he boomed. "The best. A place where I can be comfortable, *real* comfortable."

"Yes, *sir*, Mister—"

"Coglan, boy! Edsel T. Coglan. A proud name at both ends, and I'm proud to wear it!"

"Yes, *sir*, Mr. Coglan. Right away. Now let's see." He pored over his room ledgers, although, except for the Willmans and Mr. Carpenter when his wife got mad at him, there weren't any guests, as he certainly knew. He pursed his lips. He said: "Ah, good! The bridal suite's vacant, Mr. Coglan. I'm sure you'll be very comfortable there. Of course, it's eight-fifty a day."

"The bridal suite it is, boy!" Coglan chucked the pen into its holder with a fencer's thrust. He grinned like a fine old Bengal tiger with white crewcut hair.

And there was something to grin about, in a way, wasn't there? The bridal suite. That was funny.

Hardly anybody ever took the bridal suite at Pung's Inn, unless they had a bride. You only had to look at Coglan to know that he was a long way from taking a

bride—a long way, and in the wrong direction. Tall as
he was, snapping-eyed and straight-backed as he was, he
was clearly on the far side of marrying. He was at least
eighty. You could see it in his crepey skin and his gnarled
hands.

The room clerk whistled for Charley Frink. "Glad to
have you with us, Mr. Coglan," he said. "Charley'll have
your bags up in a jiffy. Will you be staying with us long?"

Coglan laughed out loud. It was the laugh of a relaxed
and confident man. "Yes," he said. "Quite long."

Now what did Coglan do when he was all alone in the
bridal suite?

Well, first he paid off the bellboy with a ten-dollar
bill. That surprised Charley Frink, all right. He wasn't
used to that kind of tipping. He went out and Coglan
closed the door behind him in a very great good humor.

Coglan was happy.

So he peered around, grinning a wolf's grin. He looked
at the bathroom, with its stall shower and bright white
porcelain. "Quaint," he murmured. He amused himself
with the electric lights, switching them on and off.
"Delicious," he said. "So *manual*." In the living room of
the suite, the main light was from an overhead six-point
chandelier, best Grand Rapids glass. Two of the pendants
were missing. "Ridiculous," chuckled old Mr. Coglan,
"but very, very sweet."

Of course, you know what he was thinking. He was
thinking of the big caverns and the big machines. He
was thinking of the design wobblators and the bomb-
shielded power sources, the self-contained raw material
lodes and the unitized distribution pipelines. But I'm getting ahead of the story. It isn't time to talk about those
things yet. So don't ask.

Anyway, after old man Coglan had a good look around,
he opened one of his bags.

He sat down in front of the desk.

He took a Kleenex out of his pocket and with a
fastidious expression picked up the blotter with it, and
dumped it on the floor.

He lifted the bag onto the bare desk top and propped
it, open, against the wall.

You never saw a bag like that! It looked like a kind

of electronic tool kit, I swear. Its back was a panel of pastel lucite with sparks embedded in it. It glittered. There was a cathode screen. There was a scanner, a microphone, a speaker. All those things and lots more. How do I know this? Why, it's all written down in a book called *My Eighteen Years at Pung's Hall*, by Senator C. T. Frink. Because Charley was in the room next door and there was a keyhole.

So then what happened was that a little tinkly chime sounded distantly within the speaker, and the cathode screen flickered and lit up.

"Coglan," boomed the tall old man. "Reporting in. Let me speak to V. P. Maffity."

II

Now you have to know what Pung's Corners was like in those days.

Everybody knows what it is now, but then it was small. Very small. It sat on the bank of the Delaware River like a fat old lady on the edge of a spindly chair.

General "Retreating Johnnie" Estabrook wintered there before the Battle of Monmouth and wrote pettishly to General Washington: "I can obtain no Provision here, as the inhabitants are so averse to our Cause, that I cannot get a Man to come near me."

During the Civil War, a small draft riot took place in its main square, in which a recruiting colonel of the IXth Volunteer Pennsylvania Zouaves was chased out of town and the son of the town's leading banker suffered superficial scalp wounds. (He fell off his horse. He was drunk.)

These were only little wars, you know. They had left only little scars.

Pung's Corners missed all the big ones.

For instance, when the biggest of all got going, why, Pung's Corners had a ticket on the fifty-yard line but never had to carry the ball.

The cobalt bomb that annihilated New Jersey stopped short at the bank of the Delaware, checked by a persistent easterly wind.

The radio-dust that demolished Philadelphia went

forty-some miles up the river. Then the drone that was spreading it was rammed down by a suicide pilot in a shaky jet. (Pung's Corners was one mile farther on.)

The H-bombs that scattered around the New York megalopolis bracketed Pung's Corners, but it lay unscathed between.

You see how it was? They never laid a glove on us. But after the war, we were marooned.

Now that wasn't a bad way to be, you know? Read some of the old books, you'll see. The way Pung's Corners felt, there was a lot to be said for being marooned. People in Pung's Corners were genuinely sorry about the war, with so many people getting killed and all. (Although we won it. It was worse for the other side.) But every cloud has its silver lining and so on, and being surrounded at every point of the compass by badlands that no one could cross had a few compensating features.

There was a Nike battalion in Pung's Corners, and they say they shot down the first couple of helicopters that tried to land because they thought they were the enemy. Maybe they did. But along about the fifth copter, they didn't think that any more, I guarantee. And then the planes stopped coming. Outside, they had plenty to think about, I suppose. They stopped bothering with Pung's Corners.

Until Mr. Coglan came in.

After Coglan got his line of communication opened up—because that was what the big suitcase was, a TV communications set—he talked for a little while. Charley had a red dent on his forehead for two days, he pressed against the doorknob so hard, trying to see.

"Mr. Maffity?" boomed Coglan, and a pretty girl's face lighted up on the screen.

"This is Vice President Maffity's secretary," she said sweetly. "I see you arrived safely. One moment, please, for Mr. Maffity."

And then the set flickered and another face showed up, the blood brother to Coglan's own. It was the face of an elderly and successful man who recognized no obstacles, the face of a man who knew what he wanted and got it. "Coglan, boy! Good to see you got there!"

"No sweat, L.S.," said Coglan. "I'm just about to secure my logistics. Money. This is going to take money."

"No trouble?"

"No trouble, Chief. I can promise you that. There isn't *going* to be any trouble." He grinned and picked up a nested set of little metallic boxes out of a pouch in the suitcase. He opened one, shook out a small disk-shaped object, silver and scarlet plastic. "I'm using this right away."

"And the reservoir?"

"I haven't checked yet, Chief. But the pilots said they dumped the stuff in. No opposition from the ground , either, did you notice that? These people used to shoot down every plane that came near. They're softening. They're ripe."

"Good enough," said L. S. Maffity from the little cathode screen. "Make it so, Coglan. Make it so."

Now, at the Shawanganunk National Bank, Mr. LaFarge saw Coglan come in and knew right away something was up.

How do I know that? Why, that's in a book too. *The Federal Budget and How I Balanced It: A Study in Surplus Dynamics*, by Treasury Secretary (Retired) Wilbur Otis LaFarge. Most everything is in a book, if you know where to look for it. That's something you young people have got to learn.

Anyway, Mr. LaFarge, who was then only an Assistant Vice President, greeted old man Coglan effusively. It was his way. "Morning, sir!" he said. "Morning! In what way can we serve you here at the bank?"

"We'll find a way," promised Mr. Coglan.

"Of course, sir. Of course!" Mr. LaFarge rubbed his hands. "You'll want a checking account. Certainly! And a savings account? And a safety deposit box? Absolutely! Christmas Club, I suppose. Perhaps a short-term auto loan, or a chattel loan on your household effects for the purpose of consolidating debts and reducing—"

"Don't have any debts," said Coglan. "Look, what's-your-name—"

"LaFarge, sir! Wilbur LaFarge. Call me Will."

"Look, Willie. Here are my credit references." And he

spilled a manila envelope out on the desk in front of LaFarge.

The banker looked at the papers and frowned. He picked one up. "Letter of credit," he said. "Some time since I saw one of those. From Danbury, Connecticut, eh?" He shook his head and pouted. "All from outside, sir."

"I'm from outside."

"I see." LaFarge sighed heavily after a second. "Well, sir, I don't know. What is it you wanted?"

"What I want is a quarter of a million dollars, Willie. In cash. And make it snappy, will you?"

Mr. LaFarge blinked.

You don't know him, of course. He was before your time. You don't know what a request like that would do to him.

When I say he blinked, I mean, man, he *blinked.* Then he blinked again and it seemed to calm him. For a moment, the veins had begun to stand out in his temples; for a moment, his mouth was open to speak. But he closed his mouth and the veins receded.

Because, you see, old man Coglan took that silvery, scarlet thing out of his pocket. It glittered. He gave it a twist and he gave it a certain kind of squeeze, and it hummed, a deep and throbbing note. But it didn't satisfy Mr. Coglan.

"Wait a minute," he said, offhandedly, and he adjusted it and squeezed it again. "That's better," he said.

The note was deeper, but still not quite deep enough to suit Coglan. He twisted the top a fraction more, until the pulsing note was too deep to be heard, and then he nodded.

There was silence for a second.

Then: "Large bills?" cried Mr. LaFarge. "Or small?" He leaped up and waved to a cashier. "Two hundred and fifty thousand dollars! You there, Tom Fairleigh! Hurry it up now. What? No, I don't care where you get it. Go out to the vault, if there isn't enough in the cages. But bring me two hundred and fifty thousand dollars!"

He sank down at his desk again, panting. "I am really sorry, sir," he apologized to Mr. Coglan. "The clerks you get these days! I almost wish that old times would come back."

"Perhaps they will, friend," said Coglan, grinning widely to himself. "Now," he said, not unkindly, "shut up."

He waited, tapping the desk top, humming to himself, staring at the blank wall. He completely ignored Mr. LaFarge until Tom Fairleigh and another teller brought four canvas sacks of bills. They began to dump them on the desk to count them.

"No, don't bother," said Coglan cheerfully, his black eyes snapping with good humor. "I trust you." He picked up the sacks, nodded courteously to Mr. LaFarge, and walked out.

Ten seconds later, Mr. LaFarge suddenly shook his head, rubbed his eyes and stared at the two tellers. "What—"

"You just gave him a quarter of a million dollars," said Tom Fairleigh. "You made me get it out of the vault."

"I *did?*"

"You did."

They looked at each other.

Mr. LaFarge said at last: "It's been a long time since we had any of *that* in Pung's Corners."

III

Now I have to tell a part that isn't so nice. It's about a girl named Marlene Groshawk. I positively will not explain any part of it. I probably shouldn't mention it at all, but it's part of the history of our country. Still—

Well, this is what happened. Yes, it's in a book too—*On Call,* by One Who Knows. (And we know who "One Who Knows" is, don't we?)

She wasn't a bad girl. Not a bit of it. Or, anyway, she didn't mean to be. She was too pretty for her own good and not very smart. What she wanted out of life was to be a television star.

Well, that was out of the question, of course. We didn't use live television at all in Pung's Corners those days, only a few old tapes. They left the commercials in, although the goods the old, dead announcers were trying to sell were not on the market anywhere, much less in

Pung's Corners. And Marlene's idol was a TV saleslady named Betty Furness. Marlene had pictures of her, dubbed off the tapes, pasted all over the walls of her room.

At the time I'm talking about, Marlene called herself a public stenographer. There wasn't too much demand for her services. (And later on, after things opened up, she gave up that part of her business entirely.) But if anybody needed a little extra help in Pung's Corners, like writing some letters or getting caught up on the back filing and such, they'd call on Marlene. She'd never worked for a stranger before.

She was rather pleased when the desk clerk told her that there was this new Mr. Coglan in town, and that he needed an assistant to help him run some new project he was up to. She didn't know what the project was, but I have to tell you that if she knew, she would have helped anyhow. Any budding TV star would, of course.

She stopped in the lobby of Pung's Inn to adjust her makeup. Charley Frink looked at her with that kind of a look, in spite of being only fifteen. She sniffed at him, tossed her head and proudly went upstairs.

She tapped on the carved oak door of Suite 41—that was the bridal suite; she knew it well—and smiled prettily for the tall old man with snapping eyes who swung it open.

"Mr. Coglan? I'm Miss Groshawk, the public stenographer. I understand you sent for me."

The old man looked at her piercingly for a moment.

"Yes," he said, "I did. Come in."

He turned his back on her and let her come in and close the door by herself.

Coglan was busy. He had the suite's television set in pieces all over the floor.

He was trying to fix it some way or another, Marlene judged. And that was odd, mused Marlene in her cloudy young way, because even if she wasn't really *brainy*, she knew that he was no television repairman, or anything like that. She knew exactly what he was. It said so on his card, and Mr. LaFarge had shown the card around town. He was a research and development counselor.

Whatever *that* was.

Marlene was conscientious, and she knew that a good public stenographer took her temporary employer's work to heart. She said: "Something wrong, Mr. Coglan?"

He looked up, irritable. "I can't get Danbury on this thing."

"Danbury, Connecticut? Outside? No, sir. It isn't supposed to get Danbury."

He straightened up and looked at her. "It isn't supposed to get Danbury." He nodded thoughtfully. "This forty-eight-inch twenty-seven tube full-color suppressed sideband UHF-VHF General Electric wall model with static suppressors and self-compensating tuning strips, it isn't supposed to get Danbury, Connecticut."

"That's right, sir."

"Well," he said, "that's going to be a big laugh on the cavern in Schenectady."

Marlene said helpfully: "It hasn't got any antenna."

Coglan frowned and corrected her. "No, that's impossible. It's got to have an antenna. These leads go somewhere."

Marlene shrugged attractively.

He said: "Right after the war, of course, you couldn't get Danbury at all. I agree. Not with all those fission products, eh? But that's down to a negligible count now. Danbury should come in loud and clear."

Marlene said: "No, it was after that. I used to, uh, date a fellow named Timmy Horan, and he was in that line of business, making television repairs, I mean. A couple years after the war, I was just a kid, they began to get pictures once in a while. Well, they passed a law, Mr. Coglan."

"A *law*?" His face looked suddenly harsh.

"Well, I think they did. Anyway, Timmy had to go around taking the antennas off all the sets. He really did. Then they hooked them up with TV tape recorders, like." She thought hard for a second. "He didn't tell me why," she volunteered.

"I know why," he said flatly.

"So it only plays records, Mr. Coglan. But if there's anything you want, the desk clerk'll get it for you. He's got lots. Dinah Shores and Jackie Gleasons and *Medic*. Oh, and Westerns. You tell him what you want."

"I see." Coglan stood there for a second, thinking. Not to her but to himself, he said: "No wonder we weren't getting through. Well, we'll see about that."

"What, Mr. Coglan?"

"Never mind, Miss Groshawk. I see the picture now. And it isn't a very pretty one."

He went back to the television set.

He wasn't a TV mechanic, no, but he knew a little something about what he was doing for sure, because he had it all back together in a minute. Oh, less than that. And not just the way it was. He had it improved. Even Marlene could see that. Maybe not *improved*, but different; he'd done something to it.

"Better?" he demanded, looking at her.

"I beg your pardon?"

"I mean does looking at the picture do anything to you?"

"I'm sorry, Mr. Coglan, but I honestly don't care for *Studio One*. It makes me think too hard, you know?"

But she obediently watched the set.

He had tuned in on the recorded wire signal that went out to all of Pung's Corners TV sets. I don't suppose you know how we did it then, but there was a central station where they ran off a show all the time, for people who didn't want to bother with tapes. It was all old stuff, of course. And everybody had seen all of them already.

But Marlene watched, and funnily, in a moment she began to giggle.

"Why, Mr. *Coglan*," she said, though he hadn't done anything at all.

"Better," he said, and he was satisfied.

He had every reason to be.

"However," said Mr. Coglan, "first things come first. I need your help."

"All right, Mr. Coglan," Marlene said in a silky voice.

"I mean in a business way. I want to hire some people. I want you to help me locate them, and to keep the records straight. Then I shall need to buy certain materials. And I'll need an office, perhaps a few buildings for light industrial purposes, and so on."

"That will take a lot of money, won't it?"

Coglan chuckled.

"Well, then," said Marlene, satisfied, "I'm your girl, Mr. Coglan. I mean in a business way. Would you mind telling me what the business is?"

"I intend to put Pung's Corners back on its feet."

"Oh, sure, Mr. Coglan. But how, I mean?"

"Advertising," said old man Coglan, with a devil's smile and a demon's voice.

Silence. There was a moment of silence.

Marlene said faintly: "I don't think they're going to like it."

"Who?"

"The bigwigs. They aren't going to like that. Not advertising, you know. I mean I'm for *you*. I'm in *favor* of advertising. I *like* it. But—"

"There's no question of liking it!" Coglan said in a terrible voice. "It's what has made our country great! It tooled us up to fight in a great war, and when that war was over, it put us back together again!"

"I understand that, Mr. Coglan," she said. "But—"

"I don't want to hear that word from you, Miss Groshawk," he snapped. "There is no question. Consider America after the war, ah? You don't remember, perhaps. They kept it from you. But the cities all were demolished. The buildings were ruins. It was only advertising that built them up again—advertising, and the power of research! For I remind you of what a great man once said: 'Our chief job in research is to keep the customer reasonably dissatisfied with what he has.' "

Coglan paused, visibly affected. "That was Charles F. Kettering of General Motors," he said, "and the beauty of it, Miss Groshawk, is that he said this in the Twenties! Imagine! So clear a perception of what Science means to all of us. So comprehensive a grasp of the meaning of American Inventiveness!"

Marlene said brokenly: "That's beautiful."

Coglan nodded. "Of course. So, you see, there is nothing at all that your bigwigs can do, like it or not. We Americans—we *real* Americans—know that without advertising there is no industry; and accordingly we have shaped advertising into a tool that serves us well. Why, here, look at that television set!"

Marlene did, and in a moment began again to giggle.
Archly she whispered: "Mr. Coglan!"

"You see? And if that doesn't suffice, well, there's always the law. Let's see what the bigwigs of Pung's Corners can do against the massed might of the United States
Army!"

"I do hope there won't be any fighting, Mr. Coglan."

"I doubt there will," he said sincerely. "And now to
work, eh? Or—" he glanced at his watch and nodded—
"after all, there's no real hurry this afternoon. Suppose we
order some dinner, just for the two of us. And some wine?
And—"

"Of course, Mr. Coglan."

Marlene started to go to the telephone, but Mr. Coglan
stopped her.

"On second thought, Miss Groshawk," he said, beginning to breathe a little hard, "I'll do the ordering. You
just sit there and rest for a minute. Watch the television
set, eh?"

IV

Now I have to tell you about Jack Tighe.

Yes, indeed. Jack Tighe. The Father of the Second
Republic. Sit tight and listen and don't interrupt, because what I have to tell you isn't exactly what you
learned in school.

The apple tree? No, that's only a story. It couldn't
have happened, you see, because apple trees don't
grow on upper Madison Avenue, and that's where Jack
Tighe spent his youth. Because Jack Tighe wasn't the
President of the Second Republic. For a long time, he
was something else, something called V.P. in charge of
S.L. division, of the advertising firm of Yust and Ruminant.

That's right. Advertising.

Don't cry. It's all right. He'd given it up, you see, long
before—oh, *long* before, even before the big war; given
it up and come to Pung's Corners, to retire.

Jack Tighe had his place out on the marshland down
at the bend of the Delaware River. It wasn't particularly
healthy there. All the highlands around Pung's Corners

drained into the creeks of that part of the area, and a lot
of radio-activity had come down. But it didn't bother
Jack Tighe, because he was too old.

He was as old as old man Coglan, in fact. And what's
more, they had known each other, back at the agency.

Jack Tighe was also big, not as big as Coglan but well
over six feet. And in a way he looked like Coglan.
You've seen his pictures. Same eyes, same devil-may-
care bounce to his walk and snap to his voice. He could
have been a big man in Pung's Corners. They would have
made him mayor any time. But he said he'd come
there to retire, and retire he would; it would take a major
upheaval to make him come out of retirement, he said.

And he got one.

The first thing was Andy Grammis, white as a sheet.

"Jack!" he whispered, out of breath at the porch steps,
for he'd run almost all the way from his store.

Jack Tighe took his feet down off the porch rail. "Sit
down, Andy," he said kindly. "I suppose I know why
you're here."

"You do, Jack?"

"I think so." Jack Tighe nodded. Oh, he was a handsome man. He said: "Aircraft dumping neoscopalamine
in the reservoir, a stranger turning up in a car with a
sheet-lead body. And we all know what's outside, don't
we? Yes, it has to be that."

"It's him, all right," babbled Andy Grammis, plopping
himself down on the steps, his face chalk. "It's him and
there's nothing we can do! He came into the store this
morning. Brought Marlene with him. We should have
done something about that girl, Jack. I knew she'd
come to no good—"

"What did he want?"

"Want? Jack, he had a pad and a pencil like he wanted
to take down *orders*, and he kept asking for—asking for
—'Breakfast foods,' he says, 'what've you got in the way
of breakfast foods?' So I told him. Oatmeal and corn
flakes. Jack, he *flew* at me! 'You don't stock Coco-
Wheet?' he says. 'Or Treets, Eets, Neets or Elixo-Wheets?
How about Hunny-Yummies, or Prune-Bran Whippets,

The Cereal with the Zip-Gun in Every Box?' 'No, sir,' I tell him.

"But he's mad by then. 'Potatoes?' he hollers. 'What about potatoes?' Well, we've got plenty of potatoes, a whole cellar full. But I tell him and *that* doesn't satisfy him. '*Raw*, you mean?' he yells. 'Not Tater-Fluff, Pre-Skortch Mickies or Uncle Everett's Converted Spuds?' And then he shows me his card."

"I know," said Jack Tighe kindly, for Grammis seemed to find it hard to go on. "You don't have to say it, if you don't want to."

"Oh, I can say it all right, Jack," said Andy Grammis bravely. "This Mr. Coglan, he's an adver—"

"No," said Jack Tighe, standing up, "don't make yourself do it. It's bad enough as it is. But it had to come. Yes, count it that it had to come, Andy. We've had a few good years, but we couldn't expect them to last forever."

"But what are we going to *do?*"

"Get up, Andy," said Jack Tighe strongly. "Come inside! Sit down and rest yourself. And I'll send for the others."

"You're going to fight him? But he has the whole United States Army behind him."

Old Jack Tighe nodded. "So he has, Andy," he said, but he seemed wonderfully cheerful.

Jack Tighe's place was a sort of ranch house, with fixings. He was a great individual man, Jack Tighe was. All of you know that, because you were taught it in school; and maybe some of you have been to the house. But it's different now; I don't care what they say. The furniture isn't just the same. And the grounds—

Well, during the big war, of course, that was where the radio-dust drained down from the hills, so nothing grew. They've prettied it up with grass and trees and flowers. Flowers! I'll tell you what's wrong with that. In his young days, Jack Tighe was an account executive on the National Floral account. Why, he wouldn't have a flower in the house, much less plant and tend them.

But it was a nice house, all the same. He fixed Andy Grammis a drink and sat him down. He phoned downtown and invited half a dozen people to come in to see

them. He didn't say what it was about, naturally. No
sense in starting a panic.

But everyone pretty much knew. The first to arrive
was Timmy Horan, the fellow from the television service, and he'd given Charley Frink a ride on the back of
his bike. He said, breathless: "Mr. Tighe, they're on our
lines. I don't know how he's done it, but Coglan is trans-
mitting on our wire TV circuit. And the stuff he's trans-
mitting, Mr. Tighe!"

"Sure," said Tighe soothingly. "Don't worry about it,
Timothy. I imagine I know what sort of stuff it is, eh?"

He got up, humming pleasantly, and snapped on the
television set. "Time for the afternoon movie, isn't it? I
suppose you left the tapes running."

"Of course, but he's interfering with it!"

Tighe nodded. "Let's see."

The picture on the TV screen quavered, twisted into
slanting lines of pale dark and snapped into shape.

"I remember that one!" Charley Frink exclaimed. "It's
one of my favorites, Timmy!"

On the screen, Number Two Son, a gun in his hand,
was backing away from a hooded killer. Number Two
Son tripped over a loose board and fell into a vat. He
came up grotesquely comic, covered with plaster and
mud.

Tighe stepped back a few paces. He spread the fingers of one hand and moved them rapidly up and down
before his eyes.

"Ah," he said, "yes. See for yourself, gentlemen."

Andy Grammis hesitatingly copied the older man. He
spread his fingers and, clumsily at first, moved them before his eyes, as though shielding his vision from the
cathode tube. Up and down he moved his hand, making
a sort of stroboscope that stopped the invisible flicker
of the racing electronic pencil.

And, yes, there it was!

Seen without the stroboscope, the screen showed
bland-faced Charlie Chan in his white Panama hat. But
the stroboscope showed something else. Between the
consecutive images of the old movie there was another
image—flashed for only a tiny fraction of a second, too

quick for the conscious brain to comprehend, but, oh, how it struck into the subconscious!

Andy blushed.

"That—that girl," he stammered, shocked. "She hasn't got any—"

"Of course she hasn't," said Tighe pleasantly. "Sub-liminal compulsion, eh? The basic sex drive; you don't know you're seeing it, but the submerged mind doesn't miss it. No. And notice the box of Prune-Bran Whippets in her hand."

Charley Frink coughed. "Now that you mention it, Mr. Tighe," he said, "I notice that I've just been thinking how tasty a dish of Prune-Bran Whippets would be right now."

"Naturally," agreed Jack Tighe. Then· he frowned. "Naked women, yes. But the female audience should be appealed to also. I wonder." He was silent for a couple of minutes, and held the others silent with him, while tirelessly he moved the spread hand before his eyes.

Then *he* blushed.

"Well," he said amiably, "that's for the female audi-ence. It's all there. Subliminal advertising. A product, and a key to the basic drives, and all flashed so quickly that the brain can't organize its defenses. So when you think of Prune-Bran Whippets, you think of sex. Or more im-portant, when you think of sex, you think of Prune-Bran Whippets."

"Gee, Mr. Tighe. I think about sex a lot."

"Everybody does," said Jack Tighe comfortingly, and he nodded.

There was a gallumphing sound from outside then and Wilbur LaFarge from the Shawanganunk National came trotting in. He was all out of breath and scared.

"He's done it again, he's done it again, Mr. Tighe, sir! That Mr. Coglan, he came and demanded more money! Said he's going to build a *real* TV network slave station here in Pung's Corners. Said he's opening up a branch agency for Yust and Ruminant, whoever they are. Said he was about to put Pung's Corners back on the map and needed money to do it."

"And you gave it to him?"

"I couldn't *help* it."

Jack Tighe nodded wisely. "No, you couldn't. Even in my day, you couldn't much help it, not when the agency had you in its sights and the finger squeezing down on the trigger. Neo-scop in the drinking water, to make every living soul in Pung's Corners a little more suggestible, a little less stiff-backed. Even me, I suppose, though perhaps I don't drink as much water as most. And subliminal advertising on the wired TV, and subsonic compulsives when it comes to man-to-man talk. Tell me, LaFarge, did you happen to hear a faint droning sound? I thought so; yes. They don't miss a trick. Well," he said, looking somehow pleased, "there's no help for it. We'll have to fight."

"Fight?" whispered Wilbur LaFarge, for he was no brave man, no, not even though he later became the Secretary of the Treasury.

"Fight!" boomed Jack Tighe.

Everybody looked at everybody else.

"There are hundreds of us," said Jack Tighe, "and there's only one of him. Yes, we'll fight! We'll distill the drinking water. We'll rip Coglan's little transmitter out of our TV circuit. Timmy can work up electronic sniffers to see what else he's using; we'll find all his gadgets, and we'll destroy them. The subsonics? Why, he has to carry that gear with him. We'll just take it away from him. It's either that or we give up our heritage as free men!"

Wilbur LaFarge cleared his throat. "And then—"

"Well you may say 'and then,'" agreed Jack Tighe. "And then the United States Cavalry comes charging over the hill to rescue him. Yes. But you must have realized by now, gentlemen, that this means war."

And so they had, though you couldn't have said that any of them seemed very happy about it.

V.

Now I have to tell you what it was like outside in those days.

The face of the Moon is no more remote. Oh, you can't imagine it, you really can't. I don't know if I can explain it to you, either, but it's all in a book and you

can read it if you want to . . . a book that was written
by somebody important, a major, who later on became a
general (but that was *much* later and in another army)
and whose name was T. Wallace Commaigne.

The book? Why, that was called *The End of the Beginning,* and it is Volume One of his twelve-volume set
of memoirs entitled: *I Served with Tighe: The Struggle
to Win the World.*

War had been coming, war that threatened more, until
it threatened everything, as the horrors in its supersonic
pouches grew beyond even the dreads of hysteria. But
there was time to guesstimate, as *Time* Magazine used
to call it.

The dispersal plan came first. Break up cities, spread
them apart, diffuse population and industry to provide
the smallest possible target for even the largest possible
bomb.

But dispersal increased another vulnerability—more
freight trains, more cargo ships, more boxcar planes carrying raw materials to and finished products from an
infinity of production points. Harder, yes, to hit and destroy, easier to choke off coming and going.

Then dig in, the planners said. Not dispersal but bomb
shelter. But more than bomb shelter—make the factories
mine for their ores, drill for their fuels, pump for their
coolants and steams—and make them independent of sup-
plies that may never be delivered, of workers who could
not live belowground for however long the unpredicta-
ble war may last, seconds or forever—even of brains that
might not reach the drawing boards and research labs
and directors' boards, brains that might either be dead
or concussed into something other than brains.

So the sub-surface factories even designed for themselves, always on a rising curve:

Against an enemy presupposed to grow smarter and
slicker and quicker with each advance, just as we and
our machines do. Against our having fewer and fewer
fighting men; pure logic that, as war continues, more
and more are killed, fewer and fewer left to operate the
killer engines. Against the destruction or capture of even
the impregnable underground factories, guarded as no
dragon of legend ever was—by all that Man could devise

at first in the way of traps and cages, blast and ray—and then by the slipleashed invention of machines ordered always to speed up—more and more, deadlier and deadlier.

And the next stage—the fortress factories hooked to each other, so that the unthinkably defended plants, should they inconceivably fall, would in the dying message pass their responsibilities to the next of kin—survivor factories to split up their work, increase output, step up the lethal pace of invention and perfection, still more murderous weapons to be operated by still fewer defenders.

And another, final plan—gear the machines to feed and house and clothe and transport a nation, a hemisphere, a world recovering from no one could know in advance what bombs and germs and poisons and—name it and it probably would happen if the war lasted long enough.

With a built-in signal of peace, of course: the air itself. Pure once more, the atmosphere, routinely tested moment by moment, would switch production from war to peace.

And so it did.

But who could have known beforehand that the machines might not *know* war from peace?

Here's Detroit: a hundred thousand rat-inhabited manless acres, blind windows and shattered walls. From the air, it is dead. But underneath it—ah, the rapid pulse of life! The hammering systole and diastole of raw-material conduits sucking in fuel and ore, pumping out finished autos. Spidery passages stretched out to the taconite beds under the Lakes. Fleets of barges issued from concrete pens to match the U-boat nests at Lorient and, unmanned, swam the Lakes and the canals to their distribution points, bearing shiny new Buicks and Plymouths.

What made them new?

Why, industrial design! For the model years changed. The Dynaflow '61 gave place to the Super-Dynaflow Mark Eight of 1962; twin-beam headlights became triple; white-wall tires turned to pastel and back to solid ebony black.

It was a matter of design efficiency.

What the Founding Fathers learned about production was essentially this: It doesn't much matter what you build, it only matters that people should want to buy it. What they learned was: Never mind the judgmatical faculties of the human race. They are a frail breed. They move no merchandise. They boost no sales. Rely, instead, on the monkey trait of curiosity.

And curiosity, of course, feeds on secrecy.

So generations of automotivators created new cosmetic gimmicks for their cars in secret laboratories staffed by sworn mutes. No atomic device was half so classified! And all Detroit echoed their security measures; fleets of canvas-swathed mysteries swarmed the highways at new-model time each year; people talked. Oh, yes—they laughed; it was comic; but though they were amused, they were piqued; it was good to make a joke of the mystery, but the capper to the joke was to own one of the new models oneself.

The appliance manufacturers pricked up their ears. Ah, so. Curiosity, eh? So they leased concealed space to design new ice-tray compartments and brought them out with a flourish of trumpets. Their refrigerators sold like mad. Yes, like mad.

RCA brooded over the lesson and added a fillip of their own; there was the vinylite record, unbreakable, colorful, new. They designed it under wraps and then, the crowning touch, they leaked the secret; it was the trick that Manhattan Project hadn't learned—a secret that concealed the real secret. For all the vinylite program was only a facade; it was security in its highest manifestation; the vinylite program was a mere cover for the submerged LP.

It moved goods. But there was a limit. The human race is a blabbermouth.

Very well, said some great unknown, eliminate the human race! Let a *machine* design the new models! Add a design unit. Set it, by means of wobblators and random-choice circuits, to make its changes in an unforeseeable way. Automate the factories; conceal them underground; program the machine to program itself. After all, why not? As Coglan had quoted Charles F. Kettering, "Our

chief job in research is to keep the customer reasonably
dissatisfied with what he has," and proper machines can
do *that* as well as any man. Better, if you really want to
know.

And so the world was full of drusy caverns from
which wonders constantly poured. The war had given
industry its start by starting the dispersal pattern; bomb
shelter had embedded the factories in rock; now industrial security made the factories independent. Goods
flowed out in a variegated torrent.

But they couldn't stop. And nobody could get inside
to shut them off or even slow them down. And that torrent of goods, made for so many people who didn't exist,
had to be moved. The advertising men had to do the
moving, and they were excellent at the job.

So that was the outside, a very, very busy place and a
very, very big one. In spite of what happened in the big
war.

I can't begin to tell you how busy it was or how big;
I can only tell you about a little bit of it. There was a
building called the Pentagon and it covered acres of
ground. It had five sides, of course; one for the Army, one
for the Navy, one for the Air Force, one for the Marines,
and one for the offices of Yust & Ruminant.

So here's the Pentagon, this great big building, the
nerve center of the United States in every way that mattered. (There was also a "Capitol," as they called it, but
that doesn't matter much. Didn't then, in fact.)

And here's Major Commaigne, in his scarlet dress uniform with his epaulettes and his little gilt sword. He's
waiting in the anteroom of the Director's Office of Yust
& Ruminant, nervously watching television. He's been
waiting there for an hour, and then at last they send for
him.

He goes in.

Don't try to imagine his emotions as he walks into
that pigskin-paneled suite. You can't. But understand
that he believes that the key to all of his future lies in
this room; he believes that with all his heart and in a
way, as it develops, he is right.

"Major," snaps an old man, a man very like Coglan
and very like Jack Tighe, for they were all pretty much

of a breed, those Ivy-League charcoal-grays, "Major, he's
coming through. It's just as we feared. There has been
trouble."

"Yes, sir!"

Major Commaigne is very erect and military in his
bearing, because he has been an Army officer for fifteen
years now and this is his first chance at combat. He
missed the big war—well, the whole Army missed the
big war; it was over too fast for moving troops—and fighting has pretty much stopped since then. It isn't *safe* to
fight, except under certain conditions. But maybe the
conditions are right now, he thinks. And it can mean a lot
to a major's career, these days, if he gets an expeditionary force to lead and acquits himself well with it!

So he stands erect, alert, sharp-eyed. His braided cap
is tucked in the corner of one arm, and his other hand
rests on the hilt of his sword, and he looks fierce. Why,
that's natural enough, too. What comes in over the TV
communicator in that pigskin-paneled office would make
any honest Army officer look fierce. The authority of the
United States has been flouted!

"L.S.," gasps the image of a tall, dark old man in the
picture tube, "they've turned against me! They've
seized my transmitter, neutralized my drugs, confiscated
my subsonic gear. All I have left is this transmitter!"

And he isn't urbane any more, this man Coglan whose
picture is being received in this room; he looks excited
and he looks mad.

"Funny," comments Mr. Maffity, called "L.S." by his
intimate staff, "that they didn't take the transmitter away
too. They must have known you'd contact us and that
there would be reprisals."

"But they *wanted* me to contact you!" cries the voice
from the picture tube. "I told them what it would mean.
L.S., they're going crazy. They're spoiling for a fight."

And after a little more talk, L.S. Maffity turns off the
set.

"We'll give it to them, eh, Major?" he says, as stern
and straight as a ramrod himself.

"We will, sir!" says the major, and he salutes, spins
around and leaves. Already he can feel the eagles on
his shoulders—who knows, maybe even stars!

And that is how the punitive expedition came to be launched; and it was exactly what Pung's Corners could have expected as a result of their actions—could have, and did.

Now I already told you that fighting had been out of fashion for some time, though getting *ready* to fight was a number-one preoccupation of a great many people. You must understand that there appeared to be no contradiction in these two contradictory facts, outside.

The big war had pretty much discouraged anybody from doing anything very violent. Fighting in the old-fashioned way—that is, with missiles and radio-dust and atomic cannon—had turned out to be expensive and for other reasons impractical. It was only the greatest of luck then that stopped things before the planet was wiped off, nice and clean, of everything more advanced than the notochord, ready for the one-celled beasts of the sea to start over again. Now things were different.

First place, all atomic explosives were under *rigid* interdiction. There were a couple of dozen countries in the world that owned A-bombs or better, and every one of them had men on duty, twenty-four hours a day, with their fingers held ready over buttons that would wipe out for once and all whichever one of them might first use an atomic weapon again. So that was out.

And aircraft, by the same token, lost a major part of their usefulness. The satellites with their beady little TV eyes scanned every place every second, so that you didn't dare drop even an ordinary HE bomb as long as some nearsighted chap watching through a satellite relay might mistake it for something nuclear—and give the order to push one of those buttons.

This left, generally speaking, the infantry.

But what infantry it was! A platoon of riflemen was twenty-three men and it owned roughly the firepower of all of Napoleon's legions. A company comprised some twelve hundred and fifty, and it could singlehanded have won World War One.

Hand weapons spat out literally sheets of metal, projectiles firing so rapidly one after another that you didn't so much try to shoot a target as to slice it in half. As far as the eye could see, a rifle bullet could fly. And where the eye was blocked by darkness, by fog or by hills, the sniperscope, the radarscreen and the pulse-beam interferometer sights could locate the target as though it were ten yards away at broad noon.

They were, that is to say, very modern weapons. In fact, the weapons that this infantry carried were so modern that half of each company was in process of learning to operate weapons that the other half had already discarded as obsolete. Who wanted a Magic-Eye Self-Aiming All-Weather Gunsight, Mark XXII, when a Mark XXIII, with Dubl-Jeweled Bearings, was available?

For it was one of the triumphs of the age that at last the planned obsolescence and high turnover of, say, a TV set or a Detroit car had been extended to carbines and bazookas.

It was wonderful and frightening to see.

It was these heroes, then, who went off to war, or to whatever might come.

Major Commaigne (so he says in his book) took a full company of men, twelve hundred and fifty strong, and started out for Pung's Corners. Air brought them to the plains of Lehigh County, burned black from radiation but no longer dangerous. From there, they journeyed by wheeled vehicles.

Major Commaigne was coldly confident. The radioactivity of the sands surrounding Pung's Corners was no problem. Not with the massive and perfect equipment he had for his force. What old Mr. Coglan could do, the United States Army could do better; Coglan drove inside sheet lead, but the expeditionary force cruised in solid iridium steel, with gamma-ray baffles fixed in place.

Each platoon had its own half-track personnel carrier. Not only did the men have their hand weapons, but each vehicle mounted a 105-mm explosive cannon, with Zip-Fire Auto-Load and Wizardtrol Safety Interlock. Fluid mountings sustained the gimbals of the cannon. Radar picked out its target. Automatic digital computers predicted and outguessed the flight of its prey.

In the lead personnel carrier, Major Commaigne barked a last word to his troops:

"This is it, men! The chips are down! You have trained
for this a long time and now you're in the middle of
it. I don't know how we're going to make out *in there—*"
and he swung an arm in the direction of Pung's Corners,
a gesture faithfully reproduced in living three-dimen-
sional color on the intercoms of each personnel carrier
in his fleet—"but win or lose, and I know we're going to
win, I want every one of you to know that you belong
to the best Company in the best Regiment of the best
Combat Infantry Team of the best Division of—"

Crump went the 105-mm piece on the lead personnel
carrier as radar range automatically sighted in and fired
upon a moving object outside, thus drowning out the
tributes he had intended to pay to Corps, to Army, to
Group and to Command.

The battle for Pung's Corners had begun.

VI

Now that first target, it wasn't any *body.*

It was only a milch cow, and one in need of freshen-
ing at that. She shouldn't have been on the baseball
field at all, but there she was, and since that was the direction from which the invader descended on the town,
she made the supreme sacrifice. Without even knowing
she'd done it, of course.

Major Commaigne snapped at his adjutant: "Lefferts!
Have the ordnance sections put the one-oh-fives on safety. Can't have this sort of thing." It had been a disagreeable sight, to see that poor old cow become hamburger,
well ketchuped, so rapidly. Better chain the big guns
until one saw, at any rate, whether Pung's Corners was
going to put up a fight.

So Major Commaigne stopped the personnel carriers
and ordered everybody out. They were past the dangerous radioactive area anyway.

The troops fell out in a handsome line of skirmish; it
was very, very fast and very, very good. From the top
of the Presbyterian Church steeple in Pung's Corners,
Jack Tighe and Andy Grammis watched through field
glasses, and I can tell you that Grammis was pretty near
hysterics. But Jack Tighe only hummed and nodded.

Major Commaigne gave an order and every man in
the line of skirmish instantly dug in. Some were in marsh
and some in mud; some had to tunnel into solid rock
and some—nearest where that first target had been—
through a thin film of beef. It didn't much matter, because they didn't use the entrenching spades of World
War II; they had Powr-Pakt Diggers that clawed into
anything in seconds, and, what's more, lined the pits
with a fine ceramic glaze. It was magnificent.

And yet, on the other hand—

Well, look. It was this way. Twenty-six personnel carriers had brought them here. Each carrier had its driver,
its relief driver, its emergency alternate driver and its
mechanic. It had its radar-and-electronics repairman,
and its radar-and-electronics repairman's assistant. It had
its ordnance staff of four, and its liaison communications
officer to man the intercom and keep in touch with the
P.C. commander.

Well, they needed all those people, of course. Couldn't
get along without them.

But that came to two hundred and eighty-two men.

Then there was the field kitchen, with its staff of forty-
seven, plus administrative detachment and dietetic staff;
the headquarters detachment, with paymaster's corps
and military police platoon; the meteorological section,
a proud sight as they began setting up their field tele-
types and fax receivers and launching their weather bal-
loons; the field hospital with eighty-one medics and
nurses, nine medical officers and attached medical administrative staff; the special services detachment,
prompt to begin setting up a three-D motion-picture
screen in the lee of the parked personnel carriers and
to commence organizing a handball tournament among
the off-duty men; the four chaplains and chaplains' as-
sistants, plus the Wisdom Counselor for Ethical Cultur-
ists, agnostics and waverers; the Historical Officer and
his eight trained clerks, already going from foxhole to
foxhole bravely carrying tape recorders, to take down
history as it was being made in the form of first-hand
impressions of the battle that had yet to be fought;
military observers from Canada, Mexico, Uruguay, the
Scandinavian Confederation and the Soviet Socialist Re-

public of Inner Mongolia, with their orderlies and at-
taches; and, of course, field correspondents from *Stars
& Stripes,* the New York *Times,* the *Christian Science
Monitor,* the Scripps-Howard chain, five wire services,
eight television networks, an independent documentary
motion-picture producer, and one hundred and twenty-
seven other newspapers and allied public information
outlets.

It was a stripped-down combat command, naturally.
Therefore, there was only one Public Information Officer per reporter.

Still . . .

Well, it left exactly forty-six riflemen in line of skirmish.

Up in the Presbyterian belfry, Andy Grammis wailed:
"Look at them, Jack! I don't know, maybe letting advertising back into Pung's Corners wouldn't be so bad. All right,
it's a rat race, but—"

"Wait," said Jack Tighe quietly, and hummed.

They couldn't see it very well, but the line of skirmish
was in some confusion. The word had been passed down
that all the field pieces had been put on safety and that
the entire firepower of the company rested in their forty-
six rifles. Well, that wasn't so bad; but after all, they
had been equipped with E-Z Fyre Revolv-a-Clip Carbines until ten days before the expeditionary force had
been mounted. Some of the troops hadn't been fully able
to familiarize themselves with the new weapons.

It went like this:

"Sam," called one private to the man in the next foxhole. "Sam, listen, I can't figure this something rifle out.
When the something green light goes on, does that mean
that the something safety is off?"

"Beats the something hell out of me," rejoined Sam,
his brow furrowed as he pored over the full-colored,
glossy-paper operating manual, alluringly entitled, *The
Five-Step Magic-Eye Way to New Combat Comfort and
Security.* "Did you see what it says here? It says, 'Magic-
Eye in Off position is provided with positive Fayl-Sayf
action, thus assuring Evr-Kleen Cartridge of dynamic

ejection and release, when used in combination with
Shoulder-Eez Anti-Recoil Pads.' "

"What did you say, Sam?"

"I said it beats the something hell out of me," said
Sam, and pitched the manual out into no-man's-land before him.

But he was sorry and immediately crept out to re-
trieve it, for although the directions seemed intended for
a world that had no relation to the rock-and-mud terra
firma around Pung's Corners, all of the step-by-step in-
structions in the manual were illustrated by mockup
photographs of starlets in Bikinis—for the cavern factories produced instruction manuals as well as weapons.
They had to, obviously, and they were good at it; the
more complicated the directions, the more photographs
they used. The vehicular ones were downright shocking.

Some minutes later: "They don't seem to be doing
anything," ventured Andy Grammis, watching from the
steeple.

"No, they don't, Andy. Well, we can't sit up here forever. Come along and we'll see what's what."

Now Andy Grammis didn't want to do that, but Jack
Tighe was a man you didn't resist very well, and so they
climbed down the winding steel stairs and picked up the
rest of the Pung's Corners Independence Volunteers, all
fourteen of them, and they started down Front Street
and out across the baseball diamond.

Twenty-six personnel carriers electronically went *ping*,
and the turrets of their one-oh-fives swiveled to zero in
on the Independence Volunteers.

Forty-six riflemen, swearing, attempted to make Akur-
A-C Greenline Sighting Strip cross Horizon Blue True-
Site Band in the Up-Close radar screens of their rifles.

And Major Commaigne, howling mad, waved a sheet
of paper under the nose of his adjutant. "What kind of
something nonsense is *this*?" he demanded, for a soldier is a soldier regardless of his rank. "I can't take those
men out of line with the enemy advancing on us!"

"Army orders, sir," said the adjutant impenetrably. He
had got his doctorate in Military Jurisprudence at Har-
vard Law and he knew whose orders meant what to

whom. "The rotation plan isn't my idea, sir. Why not take
it up with the Pentagon?"

"But, Lefferts, you idiot, I can't get through to the Pentagon! Those something newspapermen have the channels sewed up solid! And now you want me to take every
front-line rifleman out and send him to a rest camp for
three weeks—"

"No, sir," corrected the adjutant, pointing to a line in
the order. "Only for twenty days, sir, *including* travel
time. But you'd best do it right away, sir, I expect. The
order's marked 'priority.' "

Well, Major Commaigne was no fool. Never mind what
they said later. He had studied the catastrophe of Von
Paulus at Stalingrad and Lee's heaven-sent escape from
Gettysburg, and he knew what could happen to an expeditionary force in trouble in enemy territory. Even a
big one. And his, you must remember, was very small.

He knew that when you're on your own, everything
becomes your enemy; frost and diarrhea destroyed more
of the Nazi Sixth Army than the Russians did; the jolt-
ing wagons of Lee's retreat put more of his wounded and
sick out of the way than Meade's cannon. So he did
what he had to do.

"Sound the retreat!" he bawled. "We're going back to
the barn."

Retire and regroup; why not? But it wasn't as simple
as that.

The personnel carriers backed and turned like a fleet
in maneuvers. Their drivers were trained for that. But
one PC got caught in Special Service's movie screen and
blundered into another, and a flotilla of three of them
found themselves stymied by the spreading pre-fabs of
the field hospital. Five of them, doing extra duty in running electric generators from the power takeoffs at
their rear axles, were immobilized for fifteen minutes and
then boxed in.

What it came down to was that four of the twenty-six
were in shape to move right then. And obviously that
wasn't enough, so it wasn't a retreat at all; it was a disaster.

"There's only one thing to do," brooded Major Commaigne amid the turmoil, with manly tears streaming

down his face, "but how I wish I'd never tried to make lieutenant colonel!"

So Jack Tighe received Commaigne's surrender. Jack Tighe didn't act surprised. I can't say the same for the rest of the Independence Volunteers.

"No, Major, you may keep your sword," said Jack Tighe kindly. "And all of the officers may keep their Pinpoint Levl-Site No-Jolt sidearms."

"Thank you, sir," wept the major, and blundered back into the officer's club which the Headquarters Detachment had never stopped building.

Jack Tighe looked after him with a peculiar and thoughtful expression.

William LaFarge, swinging a thirty-inch hickory stick —it was all he'd been able to pick up as a weapon— babbled: "It's a great victory! Now they'll leave us alone, I bet!"

Jack Tighe didn't say a single word.

"Don't you think so, Jack? Won't they stay away now?"

Jack Tighe looked at him blankly, seemed about to answer and then turned to Charley Frink. "Charley. Listen. Don't you have a shotgun put away somewhere?"

"Yes, Mr. Tighe. And a .22. Want me to get them?"

"Why, yes, I think I do." Jack Tighe watched the youth run off. His eyes were hooded. And then he said: "Andy, do something for us. Ask the major to give us a P.O.W. driver who knows the way to the Pentagon."

And a few minutes later, Charley came back with the shotgun and the .22; and the rest, of course, is history.

THE WAGING OF THE PEACE

I

AFTER old man Tighe conquered the country (oh, now, listen. I already told you about that. Don't pester me for the same story over and over again. *You* remember about the Great March, from Pung's Corners to the Pentagon, and how Honest Jack Tighe, the Father of the Second Republic, overcame the massed might of the greatest nation of the world with a shotgun and a .22 rifle. Of course you do.)

Anyway. After old man Tighe conquered the country, things went pretty well for a while.

Oh, it was a pleasant time and a great one! He changed the world, Jack Tighe did. He took a pot of strong black coffee into his room—it was the Lincoln Study, as it was called at the time; now, of course, we know it as Tighe's Bedchamber—and sat up all one night, writing, and when the servants came wonderingly to him the next morning, there it was: the Bill of Wrongs.

See if you can remember them. Everybody learns them by heart. Surely you did too:

1. THE FIRST WRONG THAT WE MUST ABOLISH IS THE FORCED SALE OF GOODS. IN FUTURE, NO ONE SHALL SELL GOODS. VENDORS MAY ONLY PERMIT THEIR CUSTOMERS TO BUY.

2. THE SECOND WRONG THAT WE MUST ABOLISH IS ADVERTISING. ALL BILLBOARDS ARE TO BE RIPPED DOWN AT ONCE. MAGAZINES AND NEWSPAPERS WILL CONFINE THEIR PAID NOTICES TO ONE QUARTER-INCH PER PAGE, AND THESE MAY NOT HAVE ILLUSTRATIONS.

3. THE THIRD WRONG THAT WE MUST ABOLISH IS THE COMMERCIAL. ANYBODY WHO TRIES TO USE GOD'S FREE

69

AIR TIME FOR PUSHING COMMODITIES OFFERED FOR SALE IS AN ENEMY OF ALL THE PEOPLE, AND HAS TO BE EXILED TO ANTARCTICA. AT LEAST.

Why, it was the very prescription for a Golden Age! That's the way it was, and the way the people rejoiced was amazing.

Except—well, there was the matter of the factories in the caverns.

For instance, there was a man named Cossett. His first name was Archibald, but you don't have to bother remembering that part; his wife had a strong stomach, but *that* was more than she could put up with, and she mostly called him Bill. They had three kids—boys—named Chuck, Dan and Tommy, and Mrs. Cossett considered herself well off.

One morning she told her husband so: "Bill, I *love* the way Honest Jack Tighe has fixed everything up for us! Remember how it was, Bill? Remember? And now, why—well, look. Don't you notice anything?"

"Hm?" inquired Cossett.

"Your breakfast," said Essie Cossett. "Don't you like it?"

Bill Cossett looked palely at his breakfast. Orange juice, toast, coffee. He sighed deeply.

"Bill! I asked you if you *liked* it!"

"I'm eating it, aren't I? When did I ever have anything different?"

"Never, honey," his wife said gently. "You always have the same thing. But don't you notice that the toast isn't burned?"

Cossett chewed a piece of it without emotion. "That's nice," he said.

"And the coffee is fit to drink. And so's the orange juice."

Cossett said irritably: "Essie, it's *great* orange juice. It will be remembered."

Mrs. Cossett flared: "Bill, I can't say a *thing* to you in the morning without your flying *completely* off the—"

"Essie," shouted her husband, "I had a bad night!" He glared at her, a good-looking man, still young, fine father and good provider, but at the end of his rope. "I didn't sleep! Not a wink! I was awake all night, tossing and turning, tossing and turning, worrying, worrying, worrying. I'm *sorry!*" he cried, daring her to accept the apology.

"But I only—"

"Essie!"

Mrs. Cossett was wounded to the quick. Her lip quivered. Her eyes moistened. Her husband, seeing the signs, accepted defeat.

He sank back against his chair as she said meekly: "I only wanted to point out that it isn't ruined. But you're so touchy, Bill, that—I mean," she said hurriedly, "do you remember what it was like in the old days, before Jack Tighe freed us all? When every month there was a new pop-up toaster, and sometimes you had to dial each slice separately for Perfect Custom Yumminess, and sometimes a red Magic Ruby Reddy-Eye did it for you? When the coffee maker you bought in June used coarse percolator coffee grind and the one you got to replace it in September took drip?

"And now," she cried radiantly, her momentary anger forgotten, "and now I've had the same appliances for *more than six months!* I've had time to learn to use them! I can keep them until they wear out! And when they're gone, if I want I can get the exact same model again! Oh, Bill," she wept, quite overcome, "how *did* we get along in the old days, before Jack Tighe?"

Her husband pushed his chair back from the table and sat regarding her without a word for a long moment.

Then he got up, reached for his hat, groaning, "Ah, who can eat?" and rushed out of the house to his place of business.

The sign over his store read:

A. COSSETT & CO.
Authorized Buick Dealer

He sobbed all the way down to the shop.

You musn't feel too sorry for old Bill Cossett; there

were a lot like him those days. But it was pretty sad, no doubt of it.

When he got to the shop, he wanted to sob some more, but how could he, in front of the staff? One little break from him and all of them would have been wailing.

As it was, his head salesman, Harry Bull, was in a dither. He was lighting one cigarette after another, taking a single abstracted puff and placing each of them neatly, side by side like spokes, along the rim of his big glass ashtray. He didn't know he was doing it, of course. His eyes were fixed emptily on the ashtray, all right, but what his glazed vision beheld were the smoldering ashes of hellfire.

He looked up when his boss came in.

"Chief," he burst out tragically, "they've come in! The new models! I had the Springfield office on the phone a *dozen* times already this morning, I swear. But it's the same answer every time."

Cossett took a deep breath. This was a time for manhood. He stuck his chin out proudly and said, his voice perfectly level: "They won't cancel, then."

"They say they *can't*," said Harry Bull, and stared with a corpse's eyes at the crowded showroom. "They say the caverns are raising all the quotas. Sixteen more cars," he whispered dully, "and that's just the Roadmasters, Chief. I didn't tell you that part. Tomorrow we get the Specials and the Estate Wagons, and—and—

"Mr. Cossett," he wept, "the Estate Wagons are *eleven inches longer this month!* I can't stand it!" he cried wildly. "We got eighteen hundred and forty-one cars piled up already! The floor's full. The shop's full. The top two floors are full. The lot's full. We hauled all the trade-ins off to the junkyard yesterday and, even so, now we got them double-parked on both sides of the street for six blocks in every direction! You know, Chief, I couldn't even get to the place this morning? I had to park at the corner of Grand and Sterling and *walk* the rest of the way, because I couldn't get through!"

For the first time, Cossett's expression changed. "Grand and Sterling?" he repeated thoughtfully. "Yeah? I'll have to try coming that way tomorrow." Then he laughed, a bitter laugh. "One thing, Harry. Be glad we're

handling Buicks and not, you know, one of the Low-
Priced Three. I came by Culex Motors yesterday, and—
"By Godfrey," he shouted suddenly, "I'm going to go
down and talk to Manny Culex. Why not? It isn't just our
problem, Harry—it's everybody's. And maybe the whole
industry ought to get together, just for once. We never
did; nobody would start it. But things are getting to a
point where somebody's got to lead the way. Well, it's
going to be me! There just isn't any *sense* letting the
caverns turn out all these new cars after Jack Tighe has
told the whole blasted country that they don't have to
buy them any more. Washington will do something.
They'll have to!"

But all the way over to Manny Culex's, past the car-
ton-barricaded appliance stores, widely skirting the sham-
bles that surrounded the five and ten, rolling up the
windows as he threaded his way past the burst spoiled
food cans at the supermarket, Cossett couldn't put one
question out of his mind:

Suppose they couldn't?

II

Now you mustn't think Jack Tighe wasn't right on top
of this situation. He knew about it. Oh, yes! Because it
wasn't just Archibald Cossett and Manny Culex—it was
every car dealer—and it wasn't just the car dealers, but
every merchant in Rantoul who sold goods to the public; and it wasn't just Rantoul, but all of Illinois, all of
the Middle West, all the country—and, yes, when you
come right down to it, all of the world. (I mean all the
inhabited world. Naturally there was no problem in,
say, Lower Westchester.)

Things were piling up.

It was a matter of automation and salesmanship. In
the big war, it had seemed like a good idea to automate
the factories. Maybe it was—production was what count-
ed then, all kinds of production. They certainly got the
production, sure enough. Then, when the war was over,
there was a method for handling the production—a
method named advertising. But what did that mean,
when you came to think it over? It meant that people

had to be hounded into buying what they didn't really want, with money they hadn't yet earned. It meant pressure. It meant hypertension and social embarrassment and competition and confusion.

Well, Jack Tighe took care of that part, him and his famous Bill of Wrongs.

Everybody agreed that things had been intolerable before—before, that is, Tighe and his heroic band had marched on the Pentagon and set us all free. The trouble was that now advertising had been abolished and nobody felt he had to buy the new models as they came out of the big automated plants in the underground caverns . . . and what were we going to do with the products?

Jack Tighe felt that problem as keenly as any vacuum-cleaner salesman hard-selling a suburban neighborhood from door to door. He knew what the people wanted. And if he hadn't, why, he would have found it pretty quickly, because the people, in their delegations and petitions, were taking every conceivable opportunity to let him know.

For instance, there was the Midwest Motor Car Association's delegation, led by Bill Cossett, his very own self. Cossett hadn't wanted to be chairman, but he'd been the one to suggest it, and that usually carries a fixed penalty: "You thought it up? Okay. You make it go."

Jack Tighe received them in person. He listened with great courtesy and concern to their prepared speech; and that was unusual, because Tighe wasn't the relaxed old man who'd fished the Delaware south of Pung's Corners for so many happy years. No, he was an irritable President now, and delegations were nothing in his life; he faced fifty of them a day. And they all wanted the same thing. Just let us push *our* product a little, please? Naturally, no other commodity should be privileged to violate the Bill of Wrongs—nobody wants the Age of Advertising back!—but, Mr. President, the jewelry findings game (or shoes, or drugs, or business machines, or frozen food, and so forth) is historically, intrinsically, dynamically and pre-eminently *different*, because . . .

And, you'd be surprised, they all thought up reasons

to follow the "because." Some of the reasons were cork-
ers.

But Jack Tighe didn't let them get quite as far as the
reasons. He listened about a sentence and a half past the
"nobody wants the Age of Advertising back" movement
and into the broad largo that began the threnody of
their unique troubles. And then he said, with a sudden
impulse: "You there! The young fellow!"

"Cossett! Good old Bill Cossett!" cried a dozen eager
voices, as they pushed him forward.

"I'm impressed," said Jack Tighe thoughtfully, seizing
him by the hand. He had had an idea, and maybe it was
time to act on it. "I like your looks, Gossop," he said,
"and I'm going to do something for you."

"You mean you're going to let us *ad—*" began the
eager voices.

"Why, no," said Jack Tighe, surprised. "Of course not.
But I'm setting up a Committee of Activity to deal with
this situation, gentlemen. Yes, indeed. You mustn't think
we've been idle here in Washington. And I'm going to
put Artie Gossop—I mean Hassop—here on the Committee. There!" he said kindly, but proudly too. "And now,"
he added, leaving through his private door, "good day to
you all."

It was a signal honor, Bill Cossett thought, or anyway
all the eager voices assured him that it was.

But forty-eight hours later, he wasn't so sure.

The rest of the delegation had gone home. Why
wouldn't they? They had accomplished what they set out
to do. The problem was being taken care of.

But as for good old Bill Cossett, why, at that moment
he was doing the actual taking care.

And he didn't like it. It turned out that this Committee of Activity was not merely to study and make rec-
ommendations. Oh, no. That wasn't Jack Tighe's way.
The Committee was to *do* something. And for that reason, Cossett found himself with a rifle in his hand, in an
armored half track. He was part of a task force of heavy
assault troops, staring down the inclined ramp that led
to the cavern factory under Farmingdale, Long Island.

Let me tell you about Farmingdale.

National Electro-Mech had its home office there—in the

good old days, you know. Came the Cold War. The Board of Directors of National Electro-Mechanical Appliances, Inc., took a look at its balance sheet, smiled, thought of taxes, wept, and determined to plow a considerable part of its earnings into a new plant.

It was to be not merely a *new* plant, but a *fine* plant—wasn't the government paying for it anyhow, in a way? I mean what didn't come off taxes as capital expansion came back as pay for proximity-fuse contracts. So they dug themselves a great big hole—a regular underground Levittown of the machine, so to speak—acres and acres of floor surface, and all of it hidden from the light of day. Okay, chuckled the Board of Directors, rubbing its hands, let them shoot their ICBMs! Yah, Yah! Can't touch *me!*

That was during the Cold War. Well, then the Cold War hotted up, you know. The missiles flew. The Board got its orders from Washington, hurry-up orders: automate, mechanize, make it faster, boost its size. They took a deep breath and gamely sent the engineers back to the drawing boards.

The orders were to double production and make it independent of the outside world. The engineers whispered among themselves—"Are they *kidding?*" they asked—but they went to work, and as fast as the designs were approved, the construction machines went back to work to make them real.

The digging machines chugged down into the factory bays again, expanding them, making concealed tunnels; and this time they were followed by concrete-and-armorplate layers, booby-trap setters, camoufleurs, counterattack planners.

They *hid* that plant, friend. They concealed it from infra-red, ultra-violet and visual-wave spotting, from radar and sonic echo beams, from everything but the nose of a seeing-eye dog, and maybe even from that.

They *armored* it.

They fixed it so you couldn't get near it, at least not alive. They *armed* it—with homing missiles, batteries of rapid-fire weapons, everything they could think of—and they had a lot of people thinking—that would discourage intruders.

They *automated* it; not only would it make its products, but it would keep on making them as long as the
raw materials held out—yes, and change the designs, too,
because it is a basic part of industrial technology that
planned obsolescence should be built into every unit.

Yes, that was the idea. Without a man anywhere in
sight, the cavern factories could build their products,
change their designs, retool and bring out new ones.

More than that. They set sales quotas, by direct electronic hook-up with the master computer of the Bureau
of the Census in Washington; they wrote on electric type-
writers and printed on static-electricity presses all the
needed leaflets, brochures, instruction manuals and
diagrams.

Tricky problems were met with clever answers. For
instance, argued one R&D V.P., "Won't the factory
have to have at least a couple of pretty girls to use as
models for the leaflets illustrations?"

"Nah," said an engineer bluntly. "Look, Boss, here's
what we'll do."

He drew a quick and complicated schematic.

"I see," said the V.P., his eyes glazing.

Truthfully, he didn't understand at all, but then they
went ahead and built it and he saw that the thing
worked.

A memory-bank selector, informed of the need for a
picture of a pretty girl operating, say, an electric egg-
cooker, drew upon taped files of action studies of models
for the girl they wanted in the pose the computers de-
creed. Another tape supplied appropriate clothing—anything from a parka to a Bikini (mostly it was Bikinis)—
and an electronic patcher dubbed it in. A third file,
filmed on the spot, produced the egg-cooker itself,
dubbed in as large as life and twice as pretty.

It worked.

And then there was the problem of writing the manuals.

It wasn't so much the actual composition of the how-
to-do directions. There was nothing hard about *that;*
after all, the whole idea was that the consumer should
be told how to operate the thing without his having to
know what was under the chromium-plated shell. But—
well, what about trade-marked names? Some brain had

to coin the likes of Kleen-Heet Auto-Tyme Hardboyler, or Shel-Krak Puncherator.

They tried programming the computer to think that sort of thing up. The computer gulped, clucked and spewed out an assortment. The engineers looked at each other and scratched their heads. Kleen-Krak Boylerator? Eg-Sta-Tik Clocker?

Discouraged, they trailed with their reports to the V.P.

"Boss," they said, "maybe we better put this thing back on the drawing boards. These names the machine came up with don't make sense."

This time it was the V.P. who said bluntly: "Nah, don't worry. Didn't you ever hear of Hotpoint Refrigerators?"

So merrily they went on, and the cavern factories were automated.

Then, when the frantically dreaming engineers had them complete, they added one more touch.

Electric percolators need steel, chromium, copper, plastics for the extension cord, plastics for the handle, a different sort of plastic yet for the ornamental knobs and embellishments. So they supplied them—not by stockpiles, no, for stockpiles can be used up, but by telling the vast computers that ran the plant where its raw materials might be found.

They supplied National Electro-Mech with a robot-armed computer that could sniff out its raw materials and direct diggers to the lodes. They added a fusion power-plant that would run as long as its supply of fuel held out (and its fuel was hydrogen, from the water of Long Island Sound or, if that went dry, from the waters bound in the clay, the silicate sand, the very bedrock underneath).

Then they pushed the little red switch to "on," stepped back—and ducked.

Percolators came pouring out by the thousands that first day.

Then the machines began to speed up. Percolators flooded out by the tens of thousands. And then the machines settled down to full production.

"Ahem," coughed one of the engineers. "Say," he said. "I wonder. That little red button. Suppose we wanted to turn it off. *Could* we?"

Top management frowned. "Don't you know there's a war on?" they asked. "Production—that's what counts. Then, when the war is won, we can worry about turning the fool thing off. Right now, we can't take the risk that enemy agents might penetrate our defenses and cripple our war effort, so the button only works one way."

Then the war was won. And, yes, they could worry.

III

On the ramp outside Farmingdale, Major Commaigne rattled into his microphone: "Korowicz! Back me up and watch for missiles. You're air cover for the whole detachment. Bonfils, I want you on the road. Draw fire when the trucks come out, and then retire. Goodpastor, you cover the demolition crews. Gershenow, you're our reserve. Watch it now. They'll be coming out in a minute." He clicked off his microphone switch and stared, sweating, at the ramp.

Bill Cossett shifted nervously in his seat and looked at the rifle in his hand. It was a stripped-down rough-duty model, made to Jack Tighe's personal specifications, and the only thing you had to remember was that when you pulled the trigger, it would go off. But rifles weren't much a part of Cossett's life. He caught himself thinking wretchedly how nice it would be to be back in Rantoul. Then he remembered those crowded blocks of unsold Buicks.

Behind their halftrack, the four other vehicles of the party rattled into position. This ramp was one of eighteen that led from National Electro-Mech's plant to the outside world. Along it, at carefully randomed intervals, huge armored trailer-trucks rumbled up, past six sets of iridium-steel gates, out into the open air and onto the highways. No driver manned these trucks. Their orders were stamped into their circuits in the underground loading bays. Each had a destination where its load of percolators and waffle irons was to go, and each had the means of getting it there.

Bill Cossett coughed. "Major, why couldn't we just shoot them up as they come out?"

"They shoot back," said Major Commaigne.

"Yes, I know, but maybe we could use the same tactics. Automatic weapons. Let them fight it out—our robot guns against the trucks. Then—"

"Mr. Cossett," said the major wearily, "I'm glad to see you're thinking. But believe me, we've all had those thoughts." He gestured at the approaches to the ramp. "Look at those roads. You think there hasn't been plenty of fighting there?"

Cossett looked at the approaches and felt foolish. There was no doubt of it—every road for a mile around was tank-trenched, Cadmus-toothed, booby-trapped. Those were the first—and most obvious—measures the population had taken, in its early mob panic. But the trailer-trucks had been too smart for anything so simple. They had bridged the trenches, climbed the rows of dragon's teeth, and exploded the land mines harmlessly against the drum-chains that ceaselessly pounded the roads ahead of them.

"We had to stop," the major brooded, "because it just wasn't safe to live around here. The factories fight back, of course. The tougher we make it for them, the more in-genious their counterattacks and—*Stations!*" he blazed, thumbing down the microphone switch. "*Here they come!*"

The scarred outer gate whined open. A monster peered hesitantly out.

No brain—no organic brain, at least, only a maze of copper, tungsten, glass—was in it, but the truck was eerily human as it tested the air, searched its surroundings, peered radar-eyed for possible enemies. The trucks learned. They knew. There was no circuit in their elec-tronic intellects for wondering *why*, but their job was to get the merchandise delivered, and one of the sub-tasks in the job assignment was to clear the way of obstacles.

The obstacle named Major Commaigne yelled: "Hold your fire!"

Silently, their weapons hunted the vulnerable spots of axles and steering linkages on the trucks as they came out, but in each armored car, the gunners held down the interrupt buttons that kept the guns from going off. The trucks came lumbering out, flailing the roads, tur-

rets wheeling to scan the terrain around. There were
eight of them. Then:

"*Fire!*" bawled Major.Commaigne, and the battle was
on.

Bonfils, down the road, darted out of concealment and
blasted the first trucks. There was no confusion, no hesi-
tation, as the trucks regrouped and returned fire; but
Bonfils had wasted no time either, and he was out of
range in a matter of seconds.

Korowicz added his fire as the first defensive missiles
roared up. Gershenow caught two of the trucks trying to
execute a flanking movement. It was a fine, little fire
fight.

But it wasn't the main show.

"Demolition teams in!" roared Commaigne, and Goodpastor's half track bobbed up out of concealment and
landed its mining experts at the lip of the ramp itself.
The controlling machines had many circuits for directing
simultaneous activities, but the number was not infinite.
They had good reason to hope that with the active battle
out on the road, the principal guardians of the factory
might not be able to repel an attack on the entrance.

` Commaigne snapped down his gas helmet and said
thickly, through the gagging canvas and plastic: "We're
next."

Bill Cossett nodded, licked his lips and put his own
helmet on as their car circled the battle and headed for
the ramp. Before they got there, the demolition team had
blown off the first of the sets of gates. Then gray-brown
smoke still curled out, and already the demolition men
were setting their charges for the second gate, twenty
yards farther down.

"Now," said Major Commaigne, halting the halftrack
and opening the hatch. "Be careful!" he warned, leading
the detachment out, but it was hardly necessary. If they
were all like himself, Bill Cossett thought, they were
going to be careful indeed.

They marched on the heels of the demolition team
down into the automated factory.

It was noisy, and it was hot. It was dark, or nearly,
except for the lights of the demolition team and what
they carried themselves. The blasted gates were clicking

and buzzing petulantly, attempting to close themselves, aware that someone was coming through, and resenting it.

Somebody yelled: "Watch it!" and, *shwissh-poo*, a tongue of liquid butane licked out across the ramp and puffed into flame. Everybody dropped—just in time. A smell of burning wool and a yowl from Major Commaigne showed how barely in time it had been.

One of the enlisted men cried: "It's onto us! Take cover!"

But everybody had already, of course—as much as they could, not knowing just what constituted "cover" in a place that the machine-brain that ran the factory had had a solid decade to study and chart. One of the machine's built-in 37-millimeter auto-aimed guns sniffed the infrared spectrum for body heat, found it, aimed and fired.

"I'm coming, I'm coming," yammered the shells—*Vengo, vengo, vengo*—but there were blind spots around the shattered gates, and the invading party crouched in shelter.

Major Commaigne, hardly daring to raise his head, cried: "Everybody all right?"

There wasn't any answer which meant either that everybody was indeed all right . . . or dead, and thus exempted from the necessity of answering at all.

Deafened, sweltering, choking inside his anti-gas helmet, Bill Cossett swallowed hard and wished he'd kept his big mouth shut, back in Rantoul. What a committee to volunteer for!

Major Commaigne's combat boots kicked a pit in his kidneys as a .30 caliber machine-gun opened up, firing by pattern—twenty rounds at forty yards elevation and 270 degrees azimuth, traverse two degrees and fire another burst, traverse again, fire again, endlessly. It was area fire.

And it had one good feature.

"They've lost us!" Major Commaigne gloated.

The winking electronic brain inside the factory had lost sight of them—perhaps even thought they were disposed of—and was merely putting the finishing sterilizing touches on its disinfecting operation, in its meticulous machine fashion.

But Bill Cossett wasn't able to read that encouraging message out of the machine-gun fire. He didn't have the faintest idea what Major Commaigne was talking about; all he was able to tell was that the ramp was suddenly lit with a flickering light of tracer rounds, and the smell of the ammunition stifled him, and the noise of the guns and the heterodyne *squee* of the ricochets was enough to deafen. Not to mention the fact that, with all that stuff flying around, a person could get hurt.

But Major Commaigne was ready for his sneak punch. He propped himself on an elbow, very cautiously, and peered down the tunnel to where the demolition crews were rigging a larger-than-normal charge.

"Ready?" he shouted.

One of the figures waved a hand.

"Then fire!" he bawled, and the demolition men thrust down a plunger.

Warroom. A corner of the wall at the remains of the shattered gate flew out and collapsed.

Bill Cossett stared. Down from the surface was clanking a machine—an enemy? But Major Commaigne was waving it on. One of theirs then, but he had never seen it before; never seen anything like it, in fact.

And that was not surprising.

Out of heaven knows what incalculable resources, the Pentagon had produced a Winnie's Pet. The story was that back in the old days Winston Churchill—yes, that long ago!—was fighting a war against Hitler, and Churchill decided that what he needed was a trench digger of heroic proportions. A *big* one, he dreamed, big enough so that in Flanders or at Soissons, it could have turned the tide of battle.

And so his design staff produced the Winnie's Pet, a tunnel digger, huge in size. Well, maybe it would have turned the tide in 1917. But what war was ever fought in trenches again after that?

The machine was still around, though, and on the spot, because that was Major Commaigne's plan. He waved it on, into the breach in the armor-plating of the tunnel that his demolition crew had made. It was set for lateral tunneling. They gave it its head and followed it into a brand-new and therefore (presumably) unguarded tunnel that would parallel the ramp they were in, clear down to the factory itself.

Bill Cossett got up and ran after Major Commaigne and the others, unbelieving. It was all too easy! Behind them, the clatter of gunfire dwindled. There were no guns here—how could there be? They were safe.

Then—

"Ouch!" yelped Major Commaigne, inadvertently touching the wall, for it was hot. Then he grinned at Cossett, his face shadowed in the light from their helmet lamps and the tunneler. "Scared me for a minute," he said. "But it's all right. It must be fused—from the digging, you know. But—"

He stopped, thinking.

And it was only right that he should think, because he was wrong. It couldn't be atomic fusion that heated that wall. Why, Churchill didn't *have* atomic fusion to play with back in 1940, when Winnie's Pet was built!

"Run!" shouted Major Commaigne. "You, there! Get out of that thing!"

The crew hesitated, then spilled out of the digger, and again just in time.

Because the heat had been atomic, all right, but the atoms were bursting at the command of the computer that ran the factory. Seismographs had detected the vibration of their tunneling; metal subterrene moles with warheads had been sent after them; as they raced out of the new tunnel at one end, the moles burst through at the other, struck the digger and exploded.

They made it up the ramp and to their waiting halftracks, but just barely.

And that was the end of Round One. If any referee in the world had been watching, I don't care who or how biased in favor of the human race, he would have given that round to the machines. It was an easy win, no contest; and the detachment brooded about it all the way back to the Pentagon.

IV

Well, they didn't call him Unlickable Jack Tighe for nothing. In fact, they didn't call him Unlickable Jack at all then. That didn't come until later, and that's another story. But already Tighe was demonstrating the qualities which made him great.

"There's *got* to be a way," he declared, and pounded the table. "There's *got* to."

The Committee of Activity silently licked its wounds, staring at him.

"Look, fellows," Tighe said reasonably, "men built these machines. Men can make them stop!"

Bill Cossett waited for somebody else to speak. Nobody did. "How, Mr. Tighe?" he asked, wishing he didn't have to be the one to put the question.

Tighe stared fretfully—and unansweringly—out of the Pentagon window.

"You just tell us how," Cossett went on, "because we don't know. We can't get in—we've tried that. We can't blow up the goods as they come out—we've tried that too. We can't cut off the power, because it's completely self-contained. What does that leave? The computer has more resources than we have, that's all."

"There's always a way," said obstinate Jack Tighe, and shifted restlessly in his leather chair. It was not that he wasn't used to positions of responsibility, for hadn't he been on the Plans Board of Yust & Ruminant? But running a whole country was another matter.

Marlene Groshawk coughed apologetically.

"Mr. Tighe, sir," she said. (You know who Marlene Groshawk is. *Everybody* does.)

Tighe said irritably: "Later, Marlene. Can't you see this thing's got me worried?"

"But that's what it's about, Mr. Tighe," she said, "sir. I mean it's about this thing."

She put her glasses on her pretty nose and looked at her notes. She, too, had come a long way from her public-stenographer days at Pung's Corners, and it wasn't entirely an upward path. Though no doubt there was honor to being the private secretary of old Jack Tighe.

She said: "I've got it all down here, Mr. Tighe, sir. You've tried brute force and you've tried subtlety. Well, what I ask myself is this: What would that wonderful, cute old TV detective Sherlock Holmes do?"

She removed her glasses and stared thoughtfully around the room.

Major Commaigne burst out: "We could've been *killed*. But I don't mind that, Mr. Tighe. What hurts is that we failed."

Marlene said: "So what I would suggest is—"

"I can't go home and face my wife," Bill Cossett interrupted miserably. "Or all those Buicks."

"What Sher—"

Jack Tighe growled: "We'll lick it! Trust me, men. And now, unless somebody else has a suggestion, I suppose we can adjourn this meeting. God knows we've accomplished nothing. But maybe sleeping on it will help. Any objections?"

Marlene Groshawk stuck up her hand. "Mr. Tighe, sir?"

"Eh? Marlene? Well, what is it?"

She removed her glasses and looked at him piercingly. "Sherlock Holmes," she said triumphantly. "He would have got in, because he would have *disguised* himself. There! Clear as the nose on your face, when you think of it, isn't it?"

Tighe took a deep breath. He shook his head and said, with more than ordinary patience: "Marlene, please stick to taking your shorthand. Leave the rest to us."

"But really, Mr. Tighe! Sir. I mean raw materials *do* get in, don't they?"

"Well?"

"So suppose—" she said, cocking her head prettily, tapping her small white teeth with a pencil in a judgmatical way—"suppose you fellows *disguised* yourselves. *As raw materials*. And didn't sneak in, but let the factory come and get you, so to speak. How about that?"

Jack Tighe was a great and wise man, but he had a lot on his mind. He yelled: "Marlene, what's the matter with you? That's the craziest—" he hesitated—"the craziest thing I ever—" he coughed—"it's the craziest . . . What do you mean, disguise themselves?"

"I mean disguise themselves," Marlene explained earnestly. "Like *disguise*. As raw materials."

Jack Tighe was silent for a second.

Then he pounded his desk. "Love of heaven," he

cried, "I think she's got it! Captain Margate! Where's
Captain Margate? You, Commaigne! Get out of here on
the double and get me Captain Margate!"

Bill Cossett slipped quarters into the slot and waited
for his wife in Rantoul to answer her phone.

Her image took form in the screen, hair curlers and
the baggy quilted robe she liked to slop around in. But
she was still an attractive woman. "Bill? That you? But
the operator said Farmingdale."

"That's where I am, Essie. We, uh, we're going to try
something." How did you say a thing like this without
sounding heroic? It was hard, a fine line of distinction,
for what he wanted was for his wife to think he was a
hero, but not to think that he thought so too. "We're
going to, well, sneak into the cavern here."

"Sneak in?" Her voice became piercing. "Bill Cossett!
Those factories are *dangerous*. You promised me you
wouldn't get in any trouble when I let you go east!"

"Now, Essie," he soothed. "Please, Essie. It's going to
be all right. I think."

"You *think*? Bill, tell me *exactly* what you're up to!"

"No I can't!" he said, suddenly panicky, staring at the
phone as though it were an enemy. "They're all in it together, you see. The machines, I mean. I can't say over
the phone—"

"Bill!"

"But they are, Essie. We found that out. National
Electro-Mech's got a deep tunnel that goes clear to
General Motors way out in Detroit, for trucks and so on.
They get their computer parts from Philco in Phil-
adelphia. How do I know the phone isn't in on it too?
No—" he interrupted her as she was about to demand
the truth—"please, Essie. Don't ask me. How are the kids?
Chuck?"

"Skinned knee. But, Bill, you mustn't—"

"And Dan?"

"The doctor says it's only a little allergy. But I'm not
going to—"

"And Tommy?"

She frowned. "I spanked him fifty times yesterday,"
she said, an exaggeration, certainly, but at least she was

diverted from asking questions; she gave a concise catalogue of smashed dishes, spilled milk, unhung jackets and lost shoes; and Bill breathed again.

For what he told her had been the truth; he was suddenly deathly afraid that the automatic long-lines dialing apparatus of the phone company might have been infiltrated by its electronic brethren in the factories. There was no sense in telling the enemy what you were about to do!

He managed to hang up without revealing his secret, and walked out of the booth to Major Commaigne's command post.

Heroes come in many forms, but it had never before occurred to A. Cossett, Authorized Buick Dealer, that a motor-car franchise holder, like a general, must sometimes offer his life in battle.

The command post was busy, but that was natural enough, for this was a project to which the entire resources of the United States of America could well have been devoted.

And the effort was beginning to show results. Bill Cossett came to a scene of excitement. Major Commaigne was listening to an excited Captain Margate, while the rest of the detachment stood by.

Margate, as Bill Cossett had come to know, was Jack Tighe's personal expert in raw materials and the like. A good man, Cossett thought. And so was Major Commaigne a can-do kind of guy. And this Marlene Groshawk who was tagging along—well, Essie wouldn't like *that*. But it was in line of duty. And, you know, kind of fun.

Hastily, Bill Cossett shifted his thoughts back to the problem of getting into National Electro-Mech.

"Found it!" Captain Margate was crying, delighted. "We really found it! Geologists thought," he said, shaking his head in wonder, "that there wasn't any coal under Long Island, but trust the machines. They knew. We found it."

"Coal?" said Major Commaigne, his brows crinkling.

"Why, yes, Major," nodded the captain. "Coal. Raw materials, for your disguise."

"Disguise?" repeated Major Commaigne.

"That's right, Major."

"As lumps of *coal?*"

The captain shrugged cheerfully. "As organic matter," he clarified. "The machine, after all, won't mind. Coal is carbon—hydrocarbons—oh, you're close enough. The machine won't mind a few little eccentricities. Why," he went on, warming up, "the machine would still accept you even if you were a lot more impure than any of you really are."

Marlene Groshawk stamped her pretty foot. "Captain!"

"I mean in a chemical way, Miss Groshawk," the captain said humbly, and began to prepare their disguises.

Bill Cossett tugged at his collar. "Captain Margate," he said, "one thing. Suppose the factory catches us."

"It will, Mr. Cossett! That's the whole idea."

"I mean suppose it finds out we're not coal."

Captain Margate looked up thoughtfully from his pot of lampblack and cold cream.

"That," he said meditatively, "would be embarrassing. I don't know what would happen exactly, but—" He shrugged. "Still, it's not the worst thing that could happen," he added without worry. "It might be a whole lot worse if it never does find out you're not raw materials."

"You mean—" gasped Marlene. "We'd be—"

Captain Margate nodded. "You'd be processed. And," he added gallantly, "you would make a very nice batch of plastic, Miss Groshawk."

V

It was a most trying time for all of them, you may be very sure. But they were brave enough.

Major Commaigne let himself be smeared a sooty black without a flicker of his steel-gray eye or a quiver of his iron jaw.

Bill Cossett tried desperately to remember how *awful* things were back in Rantoul—"Yes, yes," he whispered frantically to himself, "even more awful than this."

Marlene Groshawk—well, you couldn't tell much from her expression. But she wrote later, in her memoirs, that she was really anxious about only one thing: How she would *ever* get all that stuff off?

Sappers had tunneled them a neat little hole into a bed of brownish gassy coal. "Ssh!" hissed Captain Margate, a finger to his lips. "Listen."

In the silence, there was a distant *chomp, chomp, chomp*, like a great far-off inchworm nibbling his way through armor-plate.

"The factory," the captain whispered. "We'll leave you now. Keep very still. Oh, and there are sandwiches and drinking water in that hamper. I don't know how long you'll have to wait."

And the captain and the sappers withdrew up the shaft.

Seconds later, a small explosive blast dumped the ceiling of the tunnel in, blocking it. The captain had warned them he would have to do that—"Don't want to make the factory suspicious, you know!"—but it was like that first clod of soil falling on the coffin of the living entombed man, all the same.

Time passed.

They ate the sandwiches and drank the water.

Time passed.

They began to get hungry again, but there wasn't anything to do about it, not any more. They couldn't even call the whole thing off now, because there wasn't any way to accomplish it. The distant *chomp, chomp* was closer, true, but the darkness was closing in on them; the enforced silence was getting on their nerves; and the sulphury smell of the low-grade coal was giving Bill Cossett a splitting headache . . .

And then it happened.

Chomp, chomp. And a *rattle, bang.* And something broke through the coal shell around them with a splash of violet light. Stainless steel teeth, half a yard long, nibbled a neat circle out of the wall, swallowed, hiccoughed and inched forward.

"Duck," whispered Major Commaigne in the girl's ear and, "Out of the way!" into Cossett's, though whispering was hardly needful in the metallic clangor around them. They crouched aside and the teeth gnawed past them, a yard a minute, trenching the floor of their little cavern

and spewing the crushed coal onto a wide conveyor belt
that followed the questing jaws.

"Jump!" murmured Commaigne when the teeth were
safely by, and the three of them leaped onto the belt,
nestled in shaking beds of coal fragments, borne upward and back toward the factory itself.

They lay quiet, hardly breathing, against what unknown spy-eyes or listening devices the factory might
employ. But if there were such, they missed their mark,
or the strategy worked. At a steady crawling pace, they
were drawn upward and into the growing din of National
Electro-Mech's main plant. It was as easy as that.

Getting *in* was. But that was, of course, only the beginning.

When National Electro-Mech put its factory under the
sod of Farmingdale, the UERMWA, Local 606, had torn
up the old contract and employed its best dreamers to
invent a new one.

"Year-round temperature of 71.5°," said Clause 14a.
"Not less than 40 cu. ft. of pure, fresh, filtered air per
worker per minute," said Paragraph 9. "Lighting to be
controlled by individual worker at his discretion," said
Sub-Section XII.

It was underground, right enough, but it was very
nice indeed. Why, they even had trouble, serious
trouble, with one worker in ten refusing to go home even
to sleep, especially during the hay-fever season.

But that was before automation had set in.

Now things were not nice at all, at least by human
standards. Machines might have loved it, but—

Well, the lights, to begin with, were hardly the pleasant, glarefree fluorescents that Local 606 had had in mind.
Why should they be? Human eyes relish the visible spectrum, but machines see by photo-electric cells, and pho-
tocells see as well by red or even infra-red . . . which is
cheap to generate and produces a satisfactory length of
filament life. Consequently National Electro-Mech was
now washed with a hideous ochre gloom.

The air—ah, that was a laugh. Whatever air the depart-
ing human workers chanced to leave behind was still
there, for machines don't breathe. And the temperature

was whatever it happened to be. In the remote ends of the galleries, it was chilly cold; in the area around the cookers, it was appalling.

And the *noise!*

Cringing, the three invaders gaped deafenedly around as they rode in on the conveyor belt. Bill Cossett stared through the blood-red gloom at a row of enormous stainless-steel spheres. He wondered what they were, and only glanced away in scant time to fling himself off the conveyor belt and yell: "Jump!"

The others obeyed just as the lumps of coal they had been traveling with thumped with a roar and suffocating dust into a huge hopper.

Beads of sweat broke out over them all. That coal was ultimately to be polymerized in the huge steel cookers Cossett had been staring at. The factory had not, of course, bothered to sweep away the excess heat with blowers. Why should it? But it wasn't only the heat that brought out the sweat; they could hear the coal being powdered and whooshed away.

They got out of there, holding hands to keep together, tripping and stumbling in the bloody dusk.

"Watch it!" bawled the major in Cossett's ear, and Cossett ducked one horrifying instant before something huge and glittering swooped by his ear.

This was, after all, an appliance factory, and Cossett couldn't help thinking that a factory should have certain recognizable features. Aisles, for example, between the machines.

But the cavern factory didn't need aisles. Most factory traffic is in the changing of the shifts, the to-and-fro traffic of the coffee break, the casual promenade to the powder room or water cooler. None of these phenomena occurred in the manless caverns. Therefore the machine-mind had ended corridors and abolished aisles. It dumped jigs and bobbins where they were most convenient—to a machine, not to a man. The movement of fresh parts and the carting away of finished assemblies was done by overhead trolleys.

As Cossett blinked after the one that had nearly whacked him, he caught glimpse of another shadow out of the corner of his eyes.

"Watch it!" he yelled, and grabbed Marlene slipperily by the neck as a pod of toasters swept by.

They all dropped to the littered floor and got up, swearing—except that Marlene didn't swear. She was much too ladylike; that is, in *that* way. But she said, "We ought to do our job and get out of here."

They looked at each other, a pathetic trio, smeared with grease and soot. They were lost in a howling, hammering catacomb. They were unarmed and helpless against a smart and powerful factory of machines and weapons.

"This was a dopy idea from the beginning," moaned Cossett. "We'll never get out."

"Never," agreed the major, daunted at last.

"Never," nodded Marlene, and paused, frowning prettily in the gloom. "Unless we get thrown up," she added.

"You mean thrown out," Cossett corrected.

Marlene shook her head. "I mean upchucked," she said in a refined manner, "like when you have an upset stomach."

The two men looked at each other.

"The place *does* eat, in a way," said Cossett.

"It's a mistake to be teleological," Commaigne objected.

"But it does eat."

"Let's think it out," said Major Commaigne authoritatively, hitting the dirt to avoid a passing coil of extension cords. "Suppose," he called up to the others, "we blow up the conveyor belt and those cookers. This will undoubtedly interfere with the logistics of the command-apparatus, right? It will then certainly try to find out what happened, and will, we must assume, discover that certain alien entities—ourselves, that is—found their way in through the raw-material receptors. Well, then! What is there for the thing to do but close down its receptors? And when it has done so, it will be cut off from the things it needs to continue manufacturing. Consequently, we may take as provisionally established, it will be unable —what?"

Bill Cossett, bawling at him from under a parts table where he had taken refuge, repeated: "I said, where's Marlene?"

The major clambered to his knees. The girl was gone. In the dull, clattering, crashing gloom, strange shapes moved wildly about, but none of them seemed to be Marlene. She was gone and, the major suddenly discovered, something was gone with her—the bag of explosives.

"Marlene!" screamed the two men.

And, though it was only chance, she at once appeared. "Where have you *been?*" the major demanded. "What were you *doing?*"

The girl stood looking down at them for a second.

"I think we'd better get out of the way," she said at last. "I took the bombs. I think I've given the thing a tummy-ache."

They had gone less than a dozen yards when the first of the little bombs went off, with a sodium-yellow glare and a firecracker bang; but it knocked a hundred yards of conveyor belt off the track.

And then the fun really began . . .

Less than an hour later, they were back on the surface, watching plumes of smoke trickle from fifty concealed ventilators scattered across the plain outside Farmingdale.

Jack Tighe was delighted. "You clobbered it!" he gloated. "And it *let* you get out?"

"*Kicked* us out," exulted the major. "We were in the raw-materials area, you know. As far as I can tell, the factory has closed down the raw-materials operation entirely. It swept everything off what was left of the conveyor belt, us included—believe me, we had to step pretty quick to keep from getting hurt! Then it plugged up the belt tunnel, and as we were getting away, I saw a handling machine beginning to put armor-plate over the plug."

Jack Tighe howled: "We've licked it! Tell you what," he said suddenly, "let's give it a *real* bellyache. Plant a few more bombs in the coal beds to make sure . . ."

And they did but, really, it didn't seem quite necessary; the cavern factory had withdrawn completely within itself. No further attempts were made to get raw materials, then or ever.

In the next few days, while Tighe's men tried the same

tactic on factory after factory, all across the face of the continent—and always with the same success—the armed guards outside National Electro-Mech's plant had very little to do. The factory wasn't quite dead, no. Twice the first day, occasionally in the days that followed, a single furtive truck would come dodging out of the exit ramps. But only one truck, where there had been scores; and that one only partly loaded, and an easy target for the guards.

It was victory.

There was no doubt about it.

Jack Tighe called for a day of national rejoicing.

VI

What a feast it was! What a celebration!

Jack Tighe was glowing with triumph and with joy. He was old and stern and powerful, but his hawk's face was the face of a delighted boy.

"Eat, my friends," he boomed, his voice rolling through the amplifiers. "Enjoy yourselves! A new day has dawned for all of us, and here are the glorious three who made it possible!"

He swept a generous arm toward those who sat beside him on the dais. Applause thundered.

The three heroes were all there. Major Commaigne sat erect, tunic crisp, buttons gleaming, a bright new scarlet ribbon over all the other ribbons on his chest, where Jack Tighe had impulsively created a new decoration on the spot. Marlene Groshawk sat beside him, radiant. Bill Cossett was stiff, grinning uncomfortably as he sat next to his wife (who was staring thoughtfully at Marlene Groshawk).

Jack Tighe bawled: "Eat, while the Marine Band plays us a march! And then we will have a few words from the heroes who have saved us all!"

It was a glorious picnic. *Hail to the Chief* bounced brassily off the bright blue sky. Cossett sat miserably, no longer stiff, wondering what the devil he would find to say, when he noticed that the brassy bugles of the Marine Corps Band faded ringingly away.

A uniformed officer had dashed breathlessly through

the crowd to the rostrum. He was whispering up to Jack Tighe, a look of tense excitement on his face.

After a moment, Tighe stood up, hands raised, a smile on his face.

"There's nothing to worry about, friends," he called, "nothing at all! But there's a *little* life in the cavern factory yet. The colonel here tells me that another truck is coming out of the ramp, that's all. So please just stay where you are and watch our boys knock it off!"

Panic? No, there wasn't any panic—why should the crowd have panicked? It was a kind of circus, an extra added attraction, as risk-free as the bear-baiting at a Sussex village fair.

Let the obstinate old factory send its trucks out, thought the assembled thousands with a joy of anticipation, it'll be fun to watch our boys smash them up! And it surely can't mean anything. The battle is won. The factories can go on plotting underground as long as they like, but you can't make toasters without copper and steel, and there hasn't been any of *that* going in for weeks. No, pure fun, that's all it is!

And so they took advantage of the spectacle, climbing on chairs to see better, the fathers lifting the youngest to their shoulders. And the truck came whooping out. *Rattle, rattle*, the machine-guns roared. *Wush* went the rocket launchers. The truck didn't have a chance. In convoys, in the old days, a few always got through; but here was only one, and it got clobbered for fair.

Bill Cossett, hand in hand with his wife, went over to look at the smoldering ruins. The crowd fell back respectfully.

Essie Cossett said gladly: "Serves them *right!* Those darn machines, they think they *own* us. I just wish I could get down there to watch them starving and suffering, like Mr. Tighe said. What are those things, dear?"

Cossett said absently: "What things?" His attention was fixed on what the bazooka charge had done to the truck's armored radiator grill, and he was thinking of how handily a rocket launcher belonging to the factory might have done the same to him.

"Those shiny things."

"*What* shiny— Oh." In the yawning flank of the truck, its steel plates sprung by half a dozen shells, a sort of metallic crate hung its edge over the lip of the hole. It was stenciled:

NATIONAL
Electro-Mech Appliances
1½ Gross Cigarette Lighters

And from a dangling flap of the crate, small, shiny globules were oozing out—dripping out, but it was odd, because the confounded things were dripping *up*. They squeezed out like water from a leaky tap, bright, striated things, and, *plop*, they were free and floated away.

"Funny," said Bill Cossett to his wife, vaguely apprehensive. "But it can't be anything to worry about. Cigarette lighters! I never saw any like that."

Wonderingly he took his own cigarette case-and-lighter combination from his pocket.

He opened it.

He held it in his hand to read the name stamped on the bottom, to see if by chance it was a National Electro-Mech.

Pflut. One of the shiny things swooped down on him, danced above the case, came toward his face. He felt a harsh, urgent thrusting at his lips, ducked, coughed, choked, nearly strangled.

Cossett scrambled to his feet, tore the cigarette out of his mouth, looked at it, threw it to the ground.

"Good God!" he cried. "But how can they? We closed them down!"

And all over the enormous crowd, others were making the same discovery, and the same error of deduction. From a smashed crate labeled *Perc-o-Matics, 8-Cup,* a shimmering series of little globes of light was whisking its way out into the air and around the crowd.

Coffee makers? Yes, they were coffee makers.

"Help!" yelled a woman whose jug of icewater was snatched out of her hands; and "Stop!" shrilled another, attempting to open a can of Maxwell House.

Coffee grounds and water swam around in the air, like the jets at Versailles drowning the brown sands of Coney

Island. Then the soggy used grounds neatly burrowed into the ground out of sight and the shimmering globe towed a sphere twice larger than itself from cup to cup, dispensing perfect coffee every time.

A four-year-old, watching with his mouth agape, absently let his ham sandwich dangle. "Ouch!" he yelled, rubbing suddenly reddened fingers as another little sphere, this one emerald green, took the bread from his hand, toasted it a golden brown, expertly caught the falling ham and restored it to him before the ham had a chance to touch the ground.

"Bill!" shrieked Essie Cossett. "What *is* this? I thought you *stopped* the factory."

"I thought so too," muttered her husband blankly, watching the frightened crowd with eyes bright with horror.

"But didn't you cut off their raw materials? Isn't that how you stopped it?"

Bill Cossett sighed. "We cut off the raw materials," he admitted. "But evidently that won't stop the factories. They're learning to do without. Force fields, magnetic flux—I don't know! But that truck was full of appliances that didn't use any raw materials at all!"

He licked dry lips. "And that's not the worst part of it," he said, so softly that his wife could hardly hear. "I can face it if the bad old days come back again. I can stand it if every three months a whole new model comes out, and we have to sell, sell, sell and buy, buy, buy. But—

"But these things," he said sickly, "don't look as though they'll ever wear out. How can they? They aren't made of matter at all! And when the new models keep coming out—*how are we ever going to get rid of the old ones?*"

THE SNOWMEN

TANDY said, "Not tonight, Howard. Why, I'm practically in bed already, see?" And she flipped the vision switch just for a second; long enough so I could get a glimpse of a sheer negligee and feathered slippers and, well, naturally, I couldn't quite believe that she *really* wanted me to stay away. Nobody made her flip that switch.

I said, "Just for a minute, Tandy. One drink. A little music, perhaps a dance——"

"Howard, you're *terrible*."

"No, dearest," I said, fast and soft and close to the phone, "I'm not terrible, I'm only very much in love. Don't say no. Don't say a word. Just close your eyes, and in ten minutes I'll be there, and—"

And then, confound them, they had to start that yapping. *Bleep-bleep* on the phone, and then: "Attention all citizens! Stand by for orders! Your world federal government has proclaimed a state of unlimited emergency. All heatpump power generators in excess of eight horsepower per—"

I slammed down the phone in disgust. Leave it to them! Yack-yack on the phone lines at all hours of the day and night, no consideration for anybody. I was disgusted, and then, when I got to thinking, not so disgusted. Why not go right over? She hadn't said no; she hadn't had a chance.

So I got the Bug out, locked the doors and set the thermostats, and I set out.

It isn't two miles to Tandy's place. Five years ago, even, I could make it in three or four minutes; now it takes ten. I call it a damned shame, though no one else seems to care. But I've always been more adventurous than most, and more social-minded. Jeffrey Otis wouldn't care about things like that. Ittel du Bois wouldn't even know—his idea is to bury his nose in a drama-tape when he goes out of the house, and let the Bug drive itself. But not me. I like to drive, even if you can't see anything and the autopilot is perfectly reliable. Life is for *living*, I say. *Live* it.

I don't pretend to understand this scientific stuff either —leave science to the people who like it, is another thing I say. But you know how when you're in your Bug and you've set the direction-finder for somebody's place, there's this *beepbeepbeepbeep* when you're going right and a *beep*SQUAWK or a SQUAWK*beep* when you go off the track? It has something to do with radio, only not radio—that's out of the question now, they say—but with sort of telephoned messages through the magma of the Earth's core. Well, that's what it says in the manual, and I know because one day I glanced through it. Anyway. Excuse me for getting technical. But I was going along toward Tandy's place, my mind full of warm pleasures and anticipating, and suddenly the *beepbeepbeep* stopped, and there was a sort of crystal chime and then a voice: "Attention! Operation of private vehicles is forbidden! Return to your home and listen to telephoned orders every hour on the hour!" And then the *beepbeepbeep* again. Why, they'd even learned how to jam the direction-finder with their confounded yapping! It was very annoying, and angrily I snapped the DF off. Daring? Yes, but I have to say that I'm an excellent driver, wonderful sense of direction, hardly need the direction-finder in the first place. And anyway we were close; the thermal pointers in the nose had already picked up Tandy's temperature gradient.

Tandy opened the locks herself. "Howard," she said in soft surprise, clutching the black film of negligee. "You really came. Oh, naughty Howard!"

"My darling!" I breathed, reaching out for her. But she dodged.

"No, Howard," she said severely, "you mustn't do that. Sit down for a moment. Have one little drink. And then

I'm going to have to be terribly stubborn and send you right home, dear."

"Of course," I said, because that was, after all, the rules of the game. "Just one drink, certainly." But, damn it, she seemed to mean it! She wasn't a bit hospitable— I mean, not *really* hospitable. She seemed friendly enough and she talked sweetly enough, but. . . . Well, for example, she sat in the positively-not chair. I can tell you a lot about the way Tandy furnished her place. There's the wing chair by the fire, and that's a bad sign because the arms are slippery and there's only room for one actually sitting in it. There's the love seat—speaks for itself, doesn't it? And there's the big sofa and, best of all, the bearskin rug. But way at the other end of the scale is this perfectly straight, armless cane-bottomed thing, with a Ming vase on one side of it and a shrub of some kind or other rooted in a bowl on the other, and that's where she sat.

I grumbled, "I shouldn't have come at all."

"What, Howard?"

"I said, uh, I couldn't come any, uh, faster. I mean, I came as fast as I could."

"I know you did, you brute," she said roguishly, and stopped the Martini-mixer. It poured us each a drink. "Now don't dawdle," she said primly. "I've got to get some sleep."

"To love," I said, and sipped the top off the Martini.

"Don't do that," she warned. I got up from the floor at her feet and went back to another chair. "You," she said, "are a hard man to handle, Howard, dear." But she giggled.

Well, you can't win them all. I finished my drink and, I don't know, I think I would have hung around about five minutes just to show who was boss and then got back in the Bug and gone home. Frankly, I was a little sleepy. It had been a wearing day, hours and hours with the orchids and then listening to all nine Beethoven symphonies in a row while I played solitaire.

But I heard the annunciator bell tinkle.

I stared at Tandy.

"My," she said prettily, "I wonder who that can be?"

"Tandy!"

"Probably someone dull," she shrugged. "I won't answer. Now, do be a good boy and——"

"Tandy! How *could* you?" My mind raced; there was only one conclusion. "Tandy, do you have Ittel du Bois coming here tonight? Don't lie to me!"

"Howard, what a *terrible* thing to say. Ittel was *last* year."

"Tell me the truth!"

"I do not!" And she was angry. I'd hurt her, no doubt of it.

"Then it must be Jeffrey. I won't stand for it. I won the toss fair and square. Why can't we wait until next year? It isn't *decent*. I—"

She stood up, her blue eyes smoldering. "Howard Mc-Guiness, you'd better go before you say something I won't be able to forgive."

I stood my ground. "Then who is it?"

"Oh, darn it," she said, and kicked viciously at the shrub by her left foot, "see for yourself. Answer the door."

So I did.

Now, I know Ittel du Bois's Bug—it's a Buick—and I know Jeff Otis's. It wasn't either one of them. The vehicle outside Tandy's door parked next to mine was a very strange looking Bug indeed. For one thing, it was only about eight feet long.

A bank of infrared lamps glowed on, bathing it in heat; the caked ice that forms in the dead spots along the hull, behind the treads and so on, melted, plopped off, turned into water and ran into the drain grille. You know how a Bug will crack and twang when it's being warmed up? They all do.

This one didn't.

It didn't make a sound. It was so silent that I could hear the snip-snip of Tandy's automatic load adjuster, throwing another heatpump into circuit to meet the drain of the infrared lamps. But no sound from the Bug outside. Also it didn't have caterpillar treads. Also it had—well, you can believe this or not—it had windows.

"You see?" said Tandy, in a voice colder than the four

miles of ice overhead. "Now would you like to apologize to me?"

"I apologize," I said in a voice that hardly got past my lips. "I—" I stopped and swallowed. I begged, "Please, Tandy, what is it?"

She lit a cigarette unsteadily. "Well, I don't rightly know. I'm kind of glad you're here, Howard," she confessed. "Maybe I shouldn't have tried to get rid of you."

"Tell me!"

She glanced at the Bug. "All right. I'll make it fast. I got a call from this, uh, fellow. I couldn't understand him very well. But. . . ."

She looked at me sidewise.

"I understand," I said. "You thought he might be a mark."

She nodded.

"And you wouldn't cut me in!" I cried angrily. "Tandy, that's mean! When I found old Buchmayr dead, didn't I cut you in on looting his place? Didn't I give you first pick of everything you wanted—except heatpumps and machine patterns, of course."

"I know, dear," she said miserably, "but—hush! He's coming out."

She was looking out the window. I looked too.

And then we looked at each other. That fellow out of the strange Bug, he was as strange as his vehicle. He might be a mark or he might not; but of one thing I was pretty sure, and that was that he wasn't human.

No. Not with huge white eyes and a serpentine frill of orange tendrils instead of hair.

At once all my lethargy and weariness vanished.

"Tandy," I cried, "he isn't human!"

"I know," she whispered.

"But don't you know what this means? He's an alien! He must come from another planet—perhaps from another star. Tandy, this is the most important thing that ever happened to us." I thought fast. "Tell you what," I said, "you let him in while I get around the side shaft— it's defrosted, isn't it? Good." I hurried. At the side door I stopped and looked at her affectionately. "Dear Tandy," I said. "And you thought this was just an ordinary mark.

You see? You *need* me." And I was off, leaving her that thought to chew on as she welcomed her visitor.

I took a good long time in the stranger's Bug. Human or monster, I could rely on Tandy to keep him occupied, so I was very thorough and didn't rush, and came out with a splendid supply of what seemed to be storage batteries. I couldn't quite make them out, but I was sure that power was in them somehow or other; and if there was power, the heatpump would find a way to suck it out. Those I took the opportunity of tucking away in my own Bug before I went back in Tandy's place. No use bothering her about them.

She was sitting in the wing chair, and the stranger was nowhere in sight. I raised my brows. She nodded. "Well," I said, "he was your guest. I won't interfere."

Tandy was looking quiet, relaxed and happy. "What about the Bug?"

"Oh, lots of things," I said. "Plenty of metal! And food —a lot of food, Tandy. Of course, we'll have to go easy on it, till we find out if we can digest it, but it smells *delicious*. And——"

"Pumps?" she demanded.

"Funny," I said. "They don't seem to use them." She scowled. "Honestly, dearest! You can see for yourself— everything I found is piled right outside the door."

"What isn't in your Bug, you mean."

"Tandy!"

She glowered a moment longer, then smiled like the sun bursting through clouds on an old video tape. "No matter, Howard," she said tenderly, "we've got plenty. Let's have another Martini, shall we?"

"Of course." I waited and took the glass. "To love," I toasted. "And to crime. By the way, did you talk to him first?"

"Oh, for *hours*," she said crossly. "Yap, yap. He's as bad as the feds."

I got up and idly walked across the room to the light switch. "Did he say anything interesting?"

"Not very. He spoke a very poor grade of English, to begin with. Said he learned it off old radio broadcasts, of all things. They float around forever out in space, it seems."

I switched off the lights. "That better?"

She nodded drowsily, got up to refill her glass, and sat down again in the love seat. "He was awfully interested in the heatpumps," she said drowsily.

I put a tape on the player—Tchaikovsky. Tandy is a fool for violins. "He liked them?"

"Oh, in a way. He thought they were clever. But dangerous, he said."

"Him and the feds," I murmured, sitting down next to her. Click-click, and our individual body armor went on stand-by alert. At the first hostile move it would block us off, set up a force field—well, I *think* it's called a force field. "The feds are always yapping about the pumps too. Did I tell you? They're even cutting in on the RDF channels now."

"Oh, Howard! That's *too* much." She sat up and got another drink—and sat, this time, on the wide, low sofa. She giggled.

"What's the matter, dear?" I asked, coming over beside her.

"He was so *funny*. Ya-ta-ta-ta, ya-ta-ta-ta, all about how the heatpumps were ruining the world."

"Just like the feds." Click-click some more, as I put my arm around her shoulders.

"Just like," she agreed. "He said it was evidently extremely high technology that produced a device that took heat out of its surrounding ambient environment, but had we ever thought of what would happen when *all* the heat was gone?"

"Crazy," I murmured into the base of her throat.

"Absolutely. As though all the heat could ever be gone! Absolute zero, he called it; said we're only eight or ten degrees from it now. That's why the snow, he said." I made a sound of polite disgust. "Yes, that's what he said. He said it wasn't just snow, it was frozen air—oxygen and nitrogen and all those things. We've frozen the Earth solid, he says, and now it's so shiny that its libido is nearly perfect."

I sat up sharply, then relaxed. "Oh. Not libido, dear. Albedo. That means it's shiny."

"That's what he said. He said the feds were right. . . .
Howard. Howard, dear. Listen to me."

"Ssh," I murmured. "Did he say anything else?"

"But Howard! Please. You're——"

"Ssh."

She relaxed, and then in a moment giggled again.
"Howard, wait. I forgot to tell you the funniest part."

It was irritating, but I could afford to be patient.
"What was that, dearest?"

"He didn't have any personal armor!"

I sat up. I couldn't help it. "What?"

"None at all! Naked as a baby. So that proves he isn't
human, doesn't it? I mean, if he can't take the simplest
care of himself, he's only a kind of animal, right?"

I thought. "Well, I suppose so," I said. Really, the con-
cept was hard to swallow.

"Good," she said, "because he's, well, in the freezer. I
didn't want to *waste* him, Howard. And it isn't as if he
was human."

I thought for a second. Well, why not? You get tired of
rabbits and mice, and since there hasn't been any open
sky for pasturing for nearly fifty years, that's about all
there is. Now that I thought back on it, he was kind of
plump and appetizing at that.

And, in any case, that was a problem for later on. I
reached out idly and touched the button that controlled
the last light in the room, the electric fireplace itself.
"Oh," I said, pausing. "Where did he come from?"

"Sorry," her muffled voice came. "I forgot to ask."

I reached out thoughtfully and found my glass. There
was a little bit left; I drained it off. Funny that the crea-
ture should bother to come down. In the old days, yes;
back when Earth was open to the sky, you might expect
aliens to come skyrocketing down from the stars and all
that. But he'd come all the way from—well, from wherever—and for what? Just to make a little soup for the pot,
to donate a little metal and power. It was funny, in a
way. I couldn't help thinking that the feds would have
liked to have met him. Not only because he agreed with
them about the pumps and so on, but because they're
interested in things like that. They're very earnest types,

that's why they're always issuing warnings and so on. Of course, nobody pays any attention.

Still. . . .

Well, there was no sense bothering my small brain about that sort of stuff, was there? If the heatpumps were dangerous, nobody would have bothered to invent them, would they?

I set down my glass and switched off the fireplace. Tandy was still and warm beside me; motionless but, believe me, by no means asleep.

THE DAY THE ICICLE WORKS CLOSED

I

THE wind was cold, pink snow was falling and Milo Pulcher had holes in his shoes. He trudged through the pink-gray slush across the square from the courthouse to the jail. The turnkey was drinking coffee out of a vinyl container. "Expecting you," he grunted. "Which one you want to see first?"

Pulcher sat down, grateful for the warmth. "It doesn't matter. Say, what kind of kids are they?"

The turnkey shrugged.

"I mean, do they give you any trouble?"

"How could they give me trouble? If they don't clean their cells they don't eat. What else they do makes no difference to me."

Pulcher took the letter from Judge Pegrim out of his pocket, and examined the list of his new clients. Avery Foltis, Walter Hopgood, Jimmy Lasser, Sam Schlesterman, Bourke Smith, Madeleine Gaultry. None of the names meant anything to him. "I'll take Foltis," he guessed, and followed the turnkey to a cell.

The Foltis boy was homely, pimply and belligerent. "Cripes," he growled shrilly, "are you the best they can do for me?"

Pulcher took his time answering. The boy was not very lovable; but, he reminded himself, there was a fifty-dollar retainer from the county for each one of these defendants, and conditions being what they were Pulcher could easily grow to love three hundred dollars. "Don't give me a hard time," he said amiably. "I may not be the best lawyer in the Galaxy, but I'm the one you've got."

"Cripes."

108

"All right, all right. Tell me what happened, will you? All I know is that you're accused of conspiracy to commit a felony, specifically an act of kidnaping a minor child."

"Yeah, that's it," the boy agreed. "You want to know what happened?" He bounced to his feet, then began acting out his story. "We were starving to death, see?" Arms clutched pathetically around his belly. "The Icicle Works closed down. Cripes, I walked the streets nearly a year, looking for something to do. Anything." Marching in place. "I even rented out for a while, but— that didn't work out." He scowled and fingered his pimply face. Pulcher nodded. Even a body-renter had to have some qualifications. The most important one was a good-looking, disease-free, strong and agile physique. "So we got together and decided, the hell, there was money to be made hooking old Swinburne's son. So—I guess we talked too much. They caught us." He gripped his wrists, like manacles.

Pulcher asked a few more questions, and then interviewed two of the other boys. He learned nothing he hadn't already known. The six youngsters had planned a reasonably competent kidnaping, and talked about it where they could be heard, and if there was any hope of getting them off it did not make itself visible to their court-appointed attorney.

Pulcher left the jail abruptly and went up the street to see Charley Dickon.

The committeeman was watching a three-way wrestling match on a flickery old TV set. "How'd it go, Milo," he greeted the lawyer, keeping his eyes on the wrestling.

Pulcher said, "I'm not going to get them off, Charley."

"Oh? Too bad." Dickon looked away from the set for the first time. "Why not?"

"They admitted the whole thing. Handwriting made the Hopgood boy on the ransom note. They all had fingerprints and cell-types all over the place. And besides, they talked too much."

Dickon said with a spark of interest, "What about Tim Lasser's son?"

"Sorry." The committeeman looked thoughtful. "I

can't help it, Charley," the lawyer protested. The kids hadn't been even routinely careful. When they planned to kidnap the son of the mayor they had talked it over, quite loudly, in a juke joint. The waitress habitually taped everything that went on in her booths. Pulcher suspected a thriving blackmail business, but that didn't change the fact that there was enough on tape to show premeditation. They had picked the mayor's son up at school. He had come with them perfectly willingly—the girl, Madeleine Gaultry, had been a babysitter for him. The boy was only three years old, but he couldn't miss an easy identification like that. And there was more: the ransom note had been sent special delivery, and young Foltis had asked the post-office clerk to put the postage on instead of using the automatic meter. The clerk remembered the pimply face very well indeed.

The committeeman sat politely while Pulcher explained, though it was obvious that most of his attention was on the snowy TV screen. "Well, Milo, that's the way it goes. Anyway, you got a fast three hundred, hey? And that reminds me."

Pulcher's guard went up.

"Here," said the committeeman, rummaging through his desk. He brought out a couple of pale green tickets. "You ought to get out and meet some more people. The Party's having its annual Chester A. Arthur Day Dinner next week. Bring your girl."

"I don't have a girl."

"Oh, you'll find one. Fifteen dollars per," explained the committeeman, handing over the tickets. Pulcher sighed and paid. Well, that was what kept the wheels oiled. And Dickon had suggested his name to Judge Pegrim. Thirty dollars out of three hundred still left him a better week's pay than he had had since the Icicle Works folded.

The committeeman carefully folded the bills into his pocket, Pulcher watching gloomily. Dickon was looking prosperous, all right. There was easily a couple of thousand in that wad. Pulcher supposed that Dickon had been caught along with everybody else on the planet when the Icicle Works folded. Nearly everybody owned stock in it, and certainly Charley Dickon, whose politician brain got him a piece of nearly every major en-

terprise on Altair Nine—a big clump of stock in the
Tourist Agency, a sizable share of the Mining Syndicate
—certainly he would have had at least a few thousand in
the Icicle Works. But it hadn't hurt him much. He
said, "None of my business, but why don't you take that
girl?"

"Madeleine Gaultry? She's in jail."

"Get her out. Here." He tossed over a bondsman's card.
Pulcher pocketed it with a scowl. That would cost another forty bucks anyway, he estimated; the bondsman
would naturally be one of Dickon's club members.

Pulcher noticed that Dickon was looking strangely
puzzled. "What's the matter?"

"Like I say, it's none of my business. But I don't get
it. You and the girl have a fight?"

"Fight? I don't even know her."

"She said you did."

"Me? No. I don't know any Madeleine Gaultry— Wait a
minute! Is that her married name? Did she used to be at
the Icicle Works?"

Dickon nodded. "Didn't you see her?"

"I didn't get to the women's wing. I—" Pulcher stood
up, oddly flustered. "Say, I'd better run along, Charley.
This bondsman, he's open now? Well—" He stopped
babbling and left.

Madeleine Gaultry! Only her name had been Madeleine
Cossett. It was funny that she should turn up now—in
jail and, Pulcher abruptly realized, likely to stay there
indefinitely. But he put that thought out of his mind;
first he wanted to see her.

The snow was turning lavender now.

Pink snow, green snow, lavender snow—any color of
the pastel rainbow. It was nothing unusual. That was
what had made Altair Nine worth colonizing in the
first place.

Now, of course, it was only a way of getting your feet
wet.

Pulcher waited impatiently at the turnkey's office while
he shambled over to the women's wing and, slowly,
returned with the girl. They looked at each other. She
didn't speak. Pulcher opened his mouth, closed it, and

silently took her by the elbow. He steered her out of the jail and hailed a cab. That was an extravagance, but he didn't care.

Madeleine shrank into a counter of the cab, looking at him out of blue eyes that were large and shadowed. She wasn't hostile, she wasn't afraid. She was only remote.

"Hungry?" She nodded. Pulcher gave the cab driver the name of a restaurant. Another extravagance, but he didn't mind the prospect of cutting down on lunches for a few weeks. He had had enough practice at it.

A year before this girl had been the prettiest secretary in the pool at the Icicle Works. He dated her half a dozen times. There was a company rule against it, but the first time it was a kind of schoolboy's prank, breaking the headmaster's regulations, and the other times it was a driving need. Then—

Then came the Gumpert Process.

That was the killer, the Gumpert Process. Whoever Gumpert was. All anybody at the Icicle Works knew was that someone named Gumpert (back on Earth, one rumor said; another said he was a colonist in the Sirian system) had come up with a cheap, practical method of synthesizing the rainbow antibiotic molds that floated free in Altair Nine's air, coloring its precipitation and, more important, providing a priceless export commodity. A whole Galaxy had depended on those rainbow molds, shipped in frozen suspensions to every inhabited planet by Altamycin, Inc.—the proper name for what everyone on Altair Nine called the Icicle Works.

When the Gumpert Process came along, suddenly the demand vanished.

Worse, the jobs vanished. Pulcher had been on the corporation's legal staff, with an office of his own and a faint hint of a vice-presidency, some day. He was out. The stenos in the pool, all but two or three of the five hundred who once had got out the correspondence and the bills, they were out. The shipping clerks in the warehouse were out, the pumphands at the settling tanks were out, the freezer attendants were out. Everyone was out. The plant closed down. There were more than fifty tons of frozen antibiotics in storage and, though there might still be a faint tickle of orders from old-fashioned

diehards around the Galaxy (backwoods country doc-
tors who didn't believe in the new-fangled synthetics,
experimenters who wanted to run comparative tests), the
shipments already en route would much more than satisfy
them. Fifty tons? Once the Icicle Works had shipped
three hundred tons a day—Physical transport, electronic
rockets that took years to cover the distance between
stars. The boom was over. And of course, on a one-
industry planet, everything else was over too.

Pulcher took the girl by the arm and swept her into
the restaurant. "Eat," he ordered. "I know what jail
food is like." He sat down, firmly determined to say
nothing until she had finished.

But he couldn't.

Long before she was ready for coffee he burst out,
"Why, Madeleine? Why would you get into something
like this?"

She looked at him but did not answer.

"What about your husband?" He didn't want to ask it,
but he had to. That had been the biggest blow of all
the unpleasant blows that had struck him after the
Icicle Works closed. Just as he was getting a law practice going—not on any big scale but, through Charley
Dickon and the Party, a small, steady handout of political favors that would make it possible for him to pretend
he was still an attorney—the gossip reached him that
Madeleine Cossett had married.

The girl pushed her plate away. "He emigrated."

Pulcher digested that slowly. Emigrated? That was the
dream of every Niner since the Works closed down, of
course. But it was only a dream. Physical transport between the stars was ungodly expensive. More, it was ungodly slow. Ten years would get you to Dell, the thin-
aired planet of a chilly little red dwarf. The nearest
good planet was thirty years away.

What it all added up to was that emigrating was almost like dying. If one member of a married couple
emigrated, it meant the end of the marriage. . . . "We got
a divorce," said Madeleine, nodding. "There wasn't enough
money for both of us to go, and Jon was unhappier here
than I was."

She took out a cigarette and let him light it. "You don't want to ask me about Jon, do you? But you want to know. All right. Jon was an artist. He was in the advertising department at the Works, but that was just temporary. He was going to do something big. Then the bottom dropped out for him, just as it did for all of us. Well, Milo, I didn't hear from you."

Pulcher protested, "It wouldn't have been *fair* for me to see you when I didn't have a job or anything."

"Of course you'd think that. It's wrong. But I couldn't find you to tell you it was wrong, and then Jon was very persistent. He was tall, curly-haired, he has a baby's face—do you know, he only shaved twice a week. Well, I married him. It lasted three months. Then he just had to get away." She leaned forward earnestly. "Don't think he was just a bum, Milo! He really was quite a good artist. But we didn't have enough money for paints, even, and then it seems that the colors are all wrong here. Jon explained it. In order to paint landscapes that sell you have to be on a planet with Earth-type colors, they're all the vogue. And there's too much altamycin in the clouds here."

Pulcher said stiffly, "I see." But he didn't, really. There was at least one unexplained part. If there hadn't been enough money for paint, then where had the money come from for a starship ticket, physical transport? It meant at least ten thousand dollars. There just was no way to raise ten thousand dollars on Altair Nine, not without taking a rather extreme step. . . .

The girl wasn't looking at him.

Her eyes were fixed on a table across the restaurant, a table with a loud, drunken party. It was only lunch time, but they had a three-o'clock-in-the-morning air about them. They were *stinking*. There were four of them, two men and two women; and their physical bodies were those of young, healthy, quite good-looking, perfectly normal Niners. The appearance of the physical bodies was entirely irrelevant, though, because they were tourists. Around the neck of each of them was a bright golden choker with a glowing red signal-jewel in the middle. It was the mark of the tourist Agency; the sign that the bodies were rented.

Milo Pulcher looked away quickly. His eyes stopped on the white face of the girl, and abruptly he knew how she had raised the money to send Jon to another star.

II

Pulcher found the girl a room and left her there. It was not what he wanted. What he wanted was to spend the evening with her and to go on spending time with her, until time came to an end: but there was the matter of her trial.

Twenty-four hours ago he had got the letter notifying him that the court had appointed him attorney for six suspected kidnapers and looked on it as a fast fee, no work to speak of, no hope for success. He would lose the case, certainly. Well, what of it?

But now he wanted to win!

It meant some fast, hard work if he was to have even a chance—and at best, he admitted to himself, the chance would not be good. Still, he wasn't going to give up without a try.

The snow stopped as he located the home of Jimmy Lasser's parents. It was a sporting-goods shop, not far from the main Tourist Agency; it had a window full of guns and boots and scuba gear. He walked in, tinkling a bell as he opened the door.

"Mr. Lasser?" A plump little man, leaning back in a chair by the door, got slowly up, looking him over.

"In back," he said shortly.

He led Pulcher behind the store, to a three-room apartment. The living room was comfortable enough, but for some reason it seemed unbalanced. One side was somehow heavier than the other. He noticed the nap of the rug, still flattened out where something heavy had been, something rectangular and large, about the size of a Tri-V electronic entertainment unit. "Repossessed," said Lasser shortly. "Sit down. Dickon called you a minute ago."

"Oh?" It had to be something important, Dickon wouldn't have tracked him down for any trivial matter.

"Don't know what he wanted, but he said you

weren't to leave till he called back. Sit down. May'll bring you a cup of tea."

Pulcher chatted with them for a minute, while the woman fussed over a teapot and a plate of soft cookies. He was trying to get the feel of the home. He could understand Madeleine Gaultry's desperation, he could understand the Foltis boy, a misfit in society anywhere. What about Jimmy Lasser?

The elder Lassers were both pushing sixty. They were first-generation Niners, off an Earth colonizing ship. They hadn't been born on Earth, of course—the trip took nearly a hundred years, physical transport. They had been born in transit, had married on the ship. As the ship had reached maximum population level shortly after they were born, they were allowed to have no children until they landed. At that time they were all of forty. May Lasser said suddenly, "Please help our boy, Mr. Pulcher! It isn't Jimmy's fault. He got in with a bad crowd. You know how it is, no work, nothing for a boy to do."

"I'll do my best." But it was funny, Pulcher thought, how it was always "the crowd" that was bad. It was never Jimmy—and never Avery, never Sam, never Walter. Pulcher sorted out the five boys and remembered Jimmy: Nineteen years old, quite colorless, polite, not very interested. What had struck the lawyer about him was only surprise that this rabbity boy should have had the enterprise to get into a criminal conspiracy in the first place.

"He's a good boy," said May Lasser pathetically. "That trouble with the parked cars two years ago wasn't his fault. He got a fine job right after that, you know. Ask his probation officer. Then the Icicle Works closed. . . ." She poured more tea, slopping it over the side of the cup. "Oh, sorry! But— But when he went to the unemployment office, Mr. Pulcher, do you know what they said to him?"

"I know."

"They asked him would he take a job if offered," she hurried on, unheeding. "A *job*. As if I didn't know what they meant by a 'job!' They meant *renting*." She plumped the teapot down on the table and began to

THE DAY THE ICICLE WORKS CLOSED 117

weep. "Mr. Pulcher, I wouldn't let him rent if I died for
it! There isn't anything in the Bible that says you can
let someone else use your body and not be responsible
for what it does! You know what tourists do! 'If thy right
hand offend thee, cut it off.' It doesn't say, unless somebody else is using it. Mr. Pulcher, renting is a *sin!*"

"May." Mr. Lasser put his teacup down and looked
directly at Pulcher. "What about it, Pulcher? Can you
get Jimmy off?"

The attorney reflected. He hadn't known about Jimmy
Lasser's probation before, and that was a bad sign. If
the county prosecutor was holding out on information of
that sort, it meant he wasn't willing to cooperate.
Probably he would be trying for a conviction with maximum sentence. Of course, he didn't have to tell a defense
attorney anything about the previous criminal records of
his clients. But in a juvenile case, where all parties were
usually willing to go easy on the defendants, it was cus-
tomary. . . . "I don't know, Mr. Lasser. I'll do the best I
can."

"Damn right you will!" barked Lasser. "Dickon tell
you who I am? I was committeeman here before him, you
know. So get busy. Pull strings. Dickon will back you,
or I'll know why!"

Pulcher managed to control himself. "I'll do the best I
can. I already told you that. If you want strings pulled,
you'd better talk to Dickon yourself. I only know law.
I don't know anything about politics."

The atmosphere was becoming unpleasant. Pulcher
was glad to hear the ringing of the phone in the store
outside. May Lasser answered it and said: "For you,
Mr. Pulcher. Charley Dickon."

Pulcher gratefully picked up the phone. Dickon's rich,
political voice said sorrowfully, "Milo? Listen, I been talking to Judge Pegrim's secretary. He isn't gonna let the
kids off with a slap on the wrist. There's a lot of heat from
the mayor's office."

Pulcher protested desperately: "But the Swinburne
kid wasn't hurt! He got better care with Madeleine than
he was getting at home."

"I know, Milo," the committeeman agreed, "but that's

the way she lies. So what I wanted to say to you, Milo, is
don't knock yourself out on this one because you
aren't going to win it."

"But—" Pulcher suddenly became aware of the Lassers
just behind him. "But I think I can get an acquittal," he
said, entirely out of hope, knowing that it wasn't true.

Dickon chuckled. "You got Lasser breathing down your
neck? Sure, Milo. But you want my advice you'll take a
quick hearing, let them get sentenced and then try for
executive clemency in a couple months. I'll help you
get it. And that's another five hundred or so for you,
see?" The committeeman was being persuasive; it was a
habit of his. "Don't worry about Lasser. I guess he's been
telling you what a power he is in politics here. Forget
it. And, say, tell him I notice he hasn't got his tickets
for the Chester A. Arthur Day Dinner yet. You pick up
the dough from him, will you? I'll mail him the tickets.
No—hold on, don't ask him. Just tell him what I said."
The connection went dead.

Pulcher stood holding a dead phone, conscious of
Lasser standing right behind him. "So long, Charley," he
said, paused, nodded into space and said, "So long,"
again.

Then the attorney turned about to deliver the committeeman's message about that most important subject,
the tickets to the Chester A. Arthur Day Dinner. Lasser
grumbled, "Damn Dickon, he's into you for one thing
after another. Where's he think I'm going to get thirty
bucks?"

"Tim. Please." His wife touched his arm.

Lasser hesitated. "Oh, all right. But you better get
Jimmy off, hear?"

Pulcher got away at last and hurried out into the cold,
slushy street.

At the corner he caught a glimpse of something palely
glowing overhead and stopped, transfixed. A huge sky-
trout was swimming purposefully down the avenue. It
was a monster, twelve feet long at least and more than
two feet thick at the middle; it would easily go eighteen,
nineteen ounces, the sort of lunker that sportsmen hiked
clear across the Dismal Hills to bag. Pulcher had never
in his life seen one that size. In fact, he could only re-

member seeing one or two fingerlings swim over inhabited areas.

It gave him a cold, worried feeling.

The skyfish were about the only tourist attraction Altair Nine had left to offer. From all over the Galaxy sports men came to shoot them, with their great porous flesh filled with bubbles of hydrogen, real biological Zeppelins that did not fly in the air but swam it. Before human colonists arrived, they had been Altair Nine's highest form of life. They were so easy to destroy with gunfire that they had almost been exterminated in the inhabited sections; only in the high, cold hills had a few survived. And now. . . .

Were even the fish aware that Altair Nine was becoming a ghost planet?

The next morning Pulcher phoned Madeleine but didn't have breakfast with her, though he wanted to very much.

He put in the whole day working on the case. In the morning he visited the families and friends of the accused boys, in the afternoon he followed a few hunches.

From the families he learned nothing. The stories were all about the same. The youngest boy was Foltis, only seventeen; the oldest was Hopgood at twenty-six. They all had lost their jobs, most of them at the Icicle Works, saw no future, and wanted off-planet. Well, physical transport meant a minimum of ten thousand dollars, and not one of them had a chance in the worlds of getting that much money in any legitimate way.

Mayor Swinburne was a rich man, and his three-year-old son was the apple of his eye. It must have been an irresistible temptation to try to collect ransom money, Pulcher realized. The mayor could certainly afford it, and once the money was collected and they were aboard a starship it would be almost impossible for the law to pursue them.

Pulcher managed to piece together the way the thing had started. The boys all lived in the same neighborhood, the neighborhood where Madeleine and Jon Gaultry had had a little apartment. They had seen Madeleine walking with the mayor's son—she had had a part-

time job, now and then, taking care of him. The only part
of the thing that was hard to believe was that Madeleine
had been willing to take part in the scheme, once the
boys approached her.

But Milo, remembering the expression on the girl's
face as she looked at the tourists, decided that wasn't so
strange after all.

For Madeleine had rented.

Physical transport was expensive and eternally slow.

But there was a faster way for a man to travel from
planet to planet—practically instantaneous, from one
end of the Galaxy to the other. The pattern of the mind
is electronic in nature. It can be taped, and it can be
broadcast on an electromagnetic frequency. What was
more, like any electromagnetic signal, it could be used
to modulate an ultrawave carrier. The result: Instantaneous transmission of personality, anywhere in the
civilized Galaxy.

The only problem was that there had to be a receiver.

The naked ghost of a man, stripped of flesh and juices,
was no more than the countless radio and TV waves
that passed through everyone all the time. The trans-
mitted personality had to be given form. There were
mechanical receivers, of course—computerlike affairs
with mercury memory cells where a man's intelligence
could be received, and could be made to activate robot
bodies. But that wasn't *fun*. The tourist trade was
built on *fun*. Live bodies were needed to satisfy the
customers. No one wanted to spend the price of a fishing
broadcast to Altair Nine in order to find himself pursuing
the quarry in some clanking tractor with photocell eyes
and solenoid muscles. A body was wanted, even a rather
attractive body; a body which would be firm where the
tourist's own, perhaps, was flabby, healthy where the
tourist's own had wheezed. Having such a body, there
were other sports to enjoy than fishing.

Oh, the laws were strict about misuse of rented bodies.

But the tourist trade was the only flourishing industry
left on Altair Nine. The laws remained strict, but they
remained unenforced.

Pulcher checked in with Charley Dickon. "I found

out why Madeleine got into this thing. She rented. Signed a long-term lease with the Tourist Agency and got a big advance on her earnings."

Dickon shook his head sadly. "What people will do for money," he commented.

"It wasn't for her! She gave it to her husband, so he could get a ticket to someplace off-world." Pulcher got up, turned around and kicked his chair as hard as he could. Renting was bad enough for a man. For a woman it was—

"Take it easy," Dickon suggested, grinning. "So she figured she could buy her way out of the contract with the money from Swinburne?"

"Wouldn't you do the same?"

"Oh, I don't know, Milo. Renting's not so bad."

"The hell it isn't!"

"All right. The hell it isn't. But you ought to realize, Milo," the committeeman said stiffly, "that if it wasn't for the tourist trade we'd all be in trouble. Don't knock the Tourist Agency. They're doing a perfectly decent job."

"Then why won't they let me see the records?"

The committeeman's eyes narrowed and he sat up straighter.

"I tried," said Pulcher. "I got them to show me Madeleine's lease agreement, but I had to threaten them with a court order. Why? Then I tried to find out a little more about the Agency itself—incorporation papers, names of shareholders and so on. They wouldn't give me a thing. Why?"

Dickon said, after a second, "I could ask you that too, Milo. Why did you want to know?"

Pulcher said seriously, "I have to make a case any way I can, Charley. They're all dead on the evidence. They're guilty. But every one of them went into this kidnaping stunt in order to stay away from renting. Maybe I can't get Judge Pegrim to listen to that kind of evidence, but maybe I can. It's my only chance. If I can show that renting is a form of cruel and unusual punishment—if I can find something wrong in it, something that isn't allowed in its charter, then I have a chance. Not a good chance. But a chance. And there's got to be some-

.thing wrong, Charley, because otherwise why would they be so secretive?"

Dickon said heavily, "You're getting in pretty deep, Milo. . . . Ever occur to you you're going about this the wrong way?"

"Wrong how?"

"What can the incorporation papers show you? You want to find out what renting's like. It seems to me the only way that makes sense is to try it yourself."

"Rent? Me?" Pulcher was shocked.

The committeeman shrugged. "Well, I got a lot to do," he said, and escorted Pulcher to the door.

The lawyer walked sullenly away. Rent? Him? But he had to admit that it made a certain amount of sense. . . .

He made a private decision. He would do what he could to get Madeleine and the others out of trouble. *Completely* out of trouble. But if, in the course of trying the case, he couldn't magic up some way of getting her out of the lease agreement as well as getting an acquittal, he would make damn sure that he didn't get the acquittal.

Jail wasn't so bad; renting, for Madeleine Gaultry, was considerably worse.

III

Pulcher marched into the unemployment office the next morning with an air of determination far exceeding what he really felt. Talk about loyalty to a client! But he had spent the whole night brooding about it, and Dickon had been right.

The clerk blinked at him and wheezed: "Gee, you're Mr. Pulcher, aren't you? I never thought I'd see *you* here. Things pretty slow?"

Pulcher's uncertainty made him belligerent. "I want to rent my body," he barked. "Am I in the right place or not?"

"Well, sure, Mr. Pulcher. I mean, you're not, if it's voluntary, but it's been so long since they had a voluntary that it don't make much difference, you know. I mean, I can handle it for you. Wait a minute." He turned away, hesitated, glanced at Pulcher and said, "I better use the other phone."

He was gone only a minute. He came back with a look of determined embarrassment. "Mr. Pulcher. Look. I thought I better call Charley Dickon. He isn't in his office. Why don't you wait until I can clear it with him?"

Pulcher said grimly, "It's already cleared with him."

The clerk hesitated. "But— Oh. All right," he said miserably, scribbling on a pad. "Right across the street. Oh, and tell them you're a volunteer. I don't know if that will make them leave the cuffs off you, but at least it'll give them a laugh." He chuckled.

Pulcher took the slip of paper and walked sternly across the street to the Tourist Rental Agency, Procurement Office, observing without pleasure that there were bars on the windows. A husky guard at the door straightened up as he approached and said genially, "All right, sonny. It isn't going to be as bad as you think. Just gimme your wrists a minute."

"Wait," said Pulcher quickly, putting his hands behind him. "You won't need the handcuffs for me. I'm a volunteer."

The guard said dangerously, "Don't kid with me, sonny." Then he took a closer look. "Hey, I know you. You're the lawyer. I saw you at the Primary Dance." He scratched his ear. He said doubtfully, "Well, maybe you are a volunteer. Go on in." But as Pulcher strutted past he felt a heavy hand on his shoulder and, click, click, his wrists were circled with steel. He whirled furiously. "No hard feelings," boomed the guard cheerfully. "It costs a lot of dough to get you ready, that's all. They don't want you changing your mind when they give you the squeeze, see?"

"The squeeze—? All right," said Pulcher, and turned away again. The squeeze. It didn't sound so good, at that. But he had a little too much pride left to ask the guard for details. Anyway, it couldn't be too bad, he was sure. Wasn't he? After all, it wasn't the same as being executed. . . .

An hour and a half later he wasn't so sure.

They had stripped him, weighed him, fluorographed him, taken samples of his blood, saliva, urine and spinal fluid; they had thumped his chest and listened to the strangled pounding of the arteries in his arm.

"All right, you pass," said a fortyish blonde in a stained nurse's uniform. "You're lucky today, openings all over. You can take your pick—mining, sailing, anything you like. What'll it be?"

"What?"

"While you're *renting*. What's the matter with you? You got to be doing something while your body's rented, you know. Of course, you can have the tank if you want to. But they mostly don't like that. You're conscious the whole time, you know."

Pulcher said honestly: "I don't know what you're talking about." But then he remembered. While a person's body was rented out there was the problem of what to do with his own mind and personality. It couldn't stay in the body. It had to go somewhere else. "The tank" was a storage device, only that and nothing more; the displaced mind was held in a sort of pickling vat of transistors and cells until its own body could be returned to it. He remembered a client of his boss's, while he was still clerking, who had spent eight weeks in the tank and had then come out to commit a murder. No. Not the tank. He said, coughing, "What else is there?"

The nurse said impatiently, "Golly, whatever you want, I guess. They've got a big call for miners operating the deep gas generators right now, if you want that. It's pretty hot, is all. They burn the coal into gas, and of course you're right in the middle of it. But I don't think you feel much. Not *too* much. I don't know about sailing or rocketing, because you have to have some experience for that. There might be something with the taxi company, but I ought to tell you usually the renters don't want that, because the live drivers don't like seeing the machines running cabs. Sometimes if they see a machine-cab they tip it over. Naturally, if there's any damage to the host machine it's risky for you."

Pulcher said faintly, "I'll try mining."

He went out of the room in a daze, a small bleached towel around his middle his only garment and hardly aware of that. His own clothes had been whisked away and checked long ago. The tourist who would shortly wear his body would pick his own clothes; the haberdashery was one of the more profitable subsidiaries of the Tourist Agency.

Then he snapped out of his daze as he discovered what was meant by "the squeeze."

A pair of husky experts lifted him onto a slab, whisked away the towel, unlocked and tossed away the handcuffs. While one pinned him down firmly at the shoulders, the other began to turn viselike wheels that moved molded forms down upon him. It was like a sectional sarcophagus closing in on him. Pulcher had an instant childhood recollection of some story or other—the walls closing in, the victim inexorably squeezed to death. He yelled, "Hey, hold it! What are you doing?"

The man at his head, bored, said, "Oh, don't worry. This your first time? We got to keep you still, you know. Scanning's close work."

"But——"

"Now shut up and relax," the man said reasonably. "If you wiggle when the tracer's scanning you you could get your whole personality messed up. Not only that, we might damage the body an' then the Agency'd have a suit on its hands, see? Tourists don't like damaged bodies. . . . Come on, Vince. Get the legs lined up so I can do the head."

"But—" said Pulcher again, and then, with effort, relaxed. It was only for twenty-four hours, after all. He could stand anything for twenty-four hours, and he had been careful to sign up for only that long. "Go ahead," he said. "It's only for twenty-four hours."

"What? Oh, sure, friend. Lights out, now; have a pleasant dream."

And something soft but quite firm came down over his face.

He heard a muffled sound of voices. Then there was a quick ripping feeling, as though he had been plucked out of some sticky surrounding medium.

Then it *hurt*.

Pulcher screamed. It didn't accomplish anything, he no longer had a voice to scream with.

Funny, he had always thought of mining as something that was carried on underground. He was under *water*.

There wasn't any doubt of it. He could see vagrant eddies of sand moving in a current; he could see real fish, not the hydrogen Zeppelins of the air; he could see bubbles, arising from some source of the sand at his feet— No! Not at his feet. He didn't have feet. He had tracks.

A great steel bug swam up in front of him and said raspingly, "All right, you there, let's go." Funny again. He didn't hear the voice with ears—he didn't have ears, and there was no stereophonic sense—but he did, somehow, hear. It seemed to be speaking inside his brain. Radio? Sonar? "Come on!" growled the bug.

Experimentally Pulcher tried to talk. "Watch it!" squeaked a thin little voice, and a tiny, many-treaded steel beetle squirmed out from under his tracks. It paused to rear back and look at him. "Dope!" it chattered scathingly. A bright flame erupted from its snout as it squirmed away.

The big bug rasped, "Go on, follow the burner, Mac." Pulcher thought of walking, rather desperately. Yes. Something was happening. He lurched and moved. "Oh, God," sighed the steel bug, hanging beside him, watching with critical attention. "This your first time? I figured. They *always* give me the new ones to break in. Look, that burner—the little thing that just went down the cline, Mac! That's a burner. It's going to burn the hard rock out of a new shaft. You follow it and pull the sludge out. With your *buckets*, Mac."

Pulcher gamely started his treads and lurchingly followed the little burner. All around him, visible through the churned, silty water, he caught glimpses of other machines working. There were big ones and little ones, some with great elephantine flexible steel trunks that sucked silt and mud away, some with wasp's stingers that planted charges of explosive, some like himself with buckets for hauling and scooping out pits. The mine, whatever sort of mine it was to be, was only a bare scratched-out beginning on the sea floor as yet. It took him—an hour? a minute? he had no means of telling time—to learn the rudiments of operating his new steel body.

Then it became boring.

Also it became painful. The first few scoops of sandy

grime he carried out of the new pit made his buckets
tingle. The tingle became a pain, the pain an ache, the
ache a blazing agony. He stopped. Something was wrong.
They couldn't expect him to go on like this! "Hey, Mac.
Get busy, will you?"

"But it *hurts.*"

"Goddamighty, Mac, it's *supposed* to hurt. How else
would you be able to feel when you hit something hard?
You want to break your buckets on me, Mac?" Pulcher
gritted his—not-teeth, squared his—not-shoulders, and
went back to digging. Ultimately the pain became,
through habit, bearable. It didn't become less. It just
became bearable.

It was boring, except when once he did strike a harder
rock than his phospher-bronze buckets could handle, and
had to slither back out of the way while the burner
chopped it up for him. But that was the only break in the
monotony. Otherwise the work was strictly routine. It
gave him plenty of time to think.

This was not altogether a boon.

I wonder, he thought with a drowned clash of buckets, I wonder what my body is doing now.

Perhaps the tenant who now occupied his body was a
businessman, Pulcher thought prayerfully. A man who
had had to come to Altair Nine quickly, on urgent business—get a contract signed, make a trading deal, arrange
an interstellar loan. That wouldn't be so bad! A businessman would not damage a rented property. No. At
the worst, a businessman might drink one or two cocktails too many, perhaps eat an indigestible lunch. All
right. So when—in surely only a few hours now—Pulcher
resumed his body, the worst he could expect would be a
hangover or dyspepsia. Well, what of that? An aspirin.
A dash of bicarb.

But maybe the tourist would not be a businessman.

Pulcher flailed the coarse sand with his buckets and
thought apprehensively: He might be a sportsman. Still,
even that wouldn't be so bad. The tourist might walk his
body up and down a few dozen mountains, perhaps even
sleep it out in the open overnight. There might be a
cold, possibly even pneumonia. Of course, there might
also be an accident—tourists did fall off the Dismal Hills;

there could be a broken leg. But that was not *too* bad, it was only a matter of a few days rest, a little medical attention.

But maybe, Pulcher thought grayly, ignoring the teeming agony of his buckets, maybe the tenant will be something worse.

He had heard queer, smutty stories about female tenants who rented male bodies. It was against the law. But you kept hearing the stories. He had heard of men who wanted to experiment with drugs, with drink, with—with a thousand secret, sordid lusts of the flesh. All of them were unpleasant. And yet in a rented body, where the ultimate price of dissipation would be borne by someone else, who might not try one of them? For there was no physical consequence to the practitioner. If Mrs. Lasser was right, perhaps there was not even a consequence in the hereafter.

Twenty-four hours had never passed so slowly.

The suction hoses squabbled with the burners. The scoops quarreled with the dynamiters. All the animate submarine mining machines constantly irritably snapped at each other. But the work was getting done.

It seemed to be a lot of work to accomplish in one twenty-four hour day, Pulcher thought seriously. The pit was down two hundred yards now, and braced. New wet-setting concrete pourers were already laying a floor. Shimmery little spiderlike machines whose limbs held chemical testing equipment were sniffing every load of sludge that came out now for richness of ore. The mine was nearly ready to start producing.

After a time Pulcher began to understand the short tempers of the machines. None of the minds in these machines were able to forget that, up topside, their bodies were going about unknown errands, risking unguessed dangers. At any given moment that concrete pourer's body, for instance, might be dying . . . might be acquiring a disease . . . might be stretched out in narcotic stupor, or might gayly be risking dismemberment in a violent sport. Naturally tempers were touchy.

There was no such thing as rest, as coffee-breaks or sleep for the machines; they kept going. Pulcher, when

finally he remembered that he had had a purpose in
coming here, it was not merely some punishment that
had come blindly to him for a forgotten sin, began to
try to analyse his own feelings and to guess at the feelings of the others.

The whole thing seemed unnecessarily *mean.* Pulcher
understood quite clearly why anyone who had had the
experience of renting would never want to do it again.
But why did it have to be so unpleasant? Surely, at least,
conditions for the renter-mind in a machine-body could
be made more bearable; the tactile sensations could be
reduced from pain to some more supportable feeling
without enough loss of sensation to jeopardize the de-
sired ends.

He wondered wistfully if Madeleine had once occupied
this particular machine.

Then he wondered how many of the dynamiters and
diggers were female, how many male. It seemed somehow
wrong that their gleaming stainless-steel or phosphor-
bronze exteriors should give no hint of age or sex. There
ought to be some lighter work for women, he thought
idly, and then realized that the thought was nonsense.
What difference did it make? You could work your buckets off, and when you got back topside you'd be healthy
and rested—

And then he had a quick, dizzying qualm, as he realized that that thought would be the thought in the
mind of the tourist now occupying his own body.

Pulcher licked his—not-lips and attacked the sand
with his buckets more viciously than before.

"All right, Mac."

The familiar steel bug was back beside him. "Come
on, back to the barn," it scolded. "You think I want to
have to haul you back? Time's up. Get the tracks back
in the parking lot."

Never was an order so gladly obeyed.

But the overseer had cut it rather fine. Pulcher had
just reached the parking space, had not quite turned
his clanking steel frame around when, *rip,* the tearing
and the pain hit him. . . .

And he found himself struggling against the enfolded
soft shroud that they called "the squeeze."

"Relax, friend," soothed a distant voice. Abruptly the pressure was removed from his face and the voice came nearer. "There you are. Have a nice dream?"

Pulcher kicked the rubbery material off his legs. He sat up.

"Ouch!" he said suddenly, and rubbed his eye.

The man by his head looked down at him and grinned. "Some shiner. Must've been a good party." He was stripping the sections of rubbery gripping material off him as he talked. "You're lucky. I've seen them come back in here with legs broken, teeth out, even bullet holes. Friend, you wouldn't believe me if I told you. 'Specially the girls." He handed Pulcher another bleached towel. "All right, you're through here. Don't worry about the eye, friend. That's easy two, three days old already. Another day or two and you won't even notice it."

"Hey!" Pulcher cried suddenly. "What do you mean, two or three days? How long was I down there?"

The man glanced boredly at the green-tabbed card on Pulcher's wrist. "Let's see, this is Thursday. Six days."

"But I only signed up for twenty-four hours!"

"Sure you did. *Plus* emergency overcalls, naturally. What do you think, friend, the Agency's going to evict some big-spending tourist just because you want your body back in twenty-four hours? Can't do it. You can see that. The Agency'd lose a fortune that way." Unceremoniously Pulcher was hoisted to his feet and escorted to the door. "If only these jokers would read the fine print," the first man was saying mournfully to his helper as Pulcher left. "Oh, well. If they had any brains they wouldn't rent in the first place—then what would me and you do for jobs?"

The closing door swallowed their laughter.

Six days! Pulcher raced through medical check-out, clothes redemption, payoff at the cashier's window. "Hurry, please," he kept saying, "can't you please hurry?" He couldn't wait to get to a phone.

But he had a pretty good idea already what the phone call would tell him. Five extra days! No wonder it had seemed so long down there, while up in the city time had passed along.

He found a phone at last and quickly dialed the pri-

vate number of Judge Pegrim's office. The judge
wouldn't be there, but that was the way Pulcher wanted
it. He got Pegrim's secretary. "Miss Kish? This is Milo
Pulcher."

Her voice was cold. "So *there* you are. Where have you
been? The judge was *furious.*"

"I—" He despaired of explaining it to her, he could
hardly explain it to himself. "I'll tell you later, Miss Kish.
Please. Where does the kidnap case stand now?"

"Why, the hearing was yesterday. Since we couldn't
locate you, the judge had to appoint another attorney.
Naturally. After all, Mr. Pulcher, an attorney is supposed
to be in court when his clients are——"

"I know that, Miss Kish. What happened?"

"It was open and shut. They all pleaded *non vult*—it
was over in twenty minutes. It was the only thing to do
on the evidence, you see. They'll be sentenced this afternoon—around three o'clock, I'd say. *If you're interested.*"

IV

It was snowing again, blue this time.

Pulcher paid the cab driver and ran up the steps of
the courthouse. As he reached for the door he caught sight
of three airfish solemnly swimming around the corner
of the building toward him. Even in his hurry he paused
to glance at them.

It was past three, but the judge had not yet entered
the courtroom. There were no spectators, but the six defendants were already in their seats, a bailiff lounging
next to them. Counsel's table was occupied by—Pulcher
squinted—oh, by Donley. Pulcher knew the other lawyer
slightly. He was a youngster, with good political con-
nections—that explained the court's appointing him for
the fee when Pulcher didn't show up—but without much
to recommend him otherwise.

Madeleine Gaultry looked up as Pulcher approached,
then looked away. One of the boys caught sight of him,
scowled, whispered to the others. Their collective ex-
pressions were enough to sear his spirit.

Pulcher sat at the table beside Donley. "Hello. Mind if
I join you?" .

Donley twisted his head. "Oh, hello, Charley. Sure. I didn't expect to see you here." He laughed. "Say, that eye's pretty bad. I guess—"

He stopped.

Something happened in Donley's face. The young baby-fat cheeks became harder, older, more worried-looking. Donley clamped his lips shut.

Pulcher was puzzled. "What's the matter? Are you wondering where I was?"

Donley said stiffly, "Well, you can't blame me for that."

"I couldn't help it, Donley. I was renting. I was trying to gather evidence—not that that helps much now. I found one thing out, though. Even a lawyer can goof in reading a contract. Did you know the Tourist Agency has the right to retain a body for up to forty-five days, regardless of the original agreement? It's in their contract. I was lucky, I guess. They only kept me five."

Donley's face did not relax. "That's interesting," he said noncommittally.

The man's attitude was most peculiar. Pulcher could understand being needled by Donley—could even understand this coldness if it had been from someone else—but it wasn't like Donley to take mere negligence so seriously.

But before he could try to pin down exactly what was wrong the other lawyer stood up. "On your feet, Pulcher," he said in a stage whisper. "Here comes the judge!"

Pulcher jumped up.

He could feel Judge Pegrim's eyes rake over him. They scratched like diamond-tipped drills. In an ordinarily political, reasonably corrupt community, Judge Pegrim was one man who took his job seriously and expected the same from those around him. "Mr. Pulcher," he purred. "We're honored to have you with us."

Pulcher began an explanation but the judge waved it away. "Mr. Pulcher, you know that an attorney is an officer of the court? And, as such, is expected to know his duties—and to fulfill them?"

"Well, Your Honor. I thought I was fulfilling them. I—"

"I'll discuss it with you at another time, Mr. Pulcher,"

the judge said. "Right now we have a rather disagreeable task to get through. Bailiff! Let's get started."

It was all over in ten minutes. Donley made a couple of routine motions, but there was no question about what would happen. It happened. Each of the defendants drew a ten-year sentence. The judge pronounced it distastefully, adjourned the court and left. He did not look at Milo Pulcher.

Pulcher tried for a moment to catch Madeleine's eye. Then he succeeded. Shaken, he turned away, bumping into Donley. "I don't understand it," he mumbled.

"What don't you understand?"

"Well, don't you think that's a pretty stiff sentence?"

Donley shrugged. He wasn't very interested. Pulcher scanned the masklike young face. There was no sympathy there. It was funny, in a way. This was a face of flint; the plight of six young people, doomed to spend a decade each of their lives in prison, did not move him at all. Pulcher said dispiritedly, "I think I'll go see Charley Dickon."

"Do that," said Donley curtly, and turned away.

But Pulcher couldn't find Charley Dickon.

He wasn't at his office, wasn't at the club. "Nope," said the garrulous retired police lieutenant who was the club president—and who used the club headquarters as a checker salon. "I haven't seen Charley in a couple of days. Be at the dinner tonight, though. You'll see him there." It wasn't a question, whether Pulcher would be at the dinner or not; Pop Craig knew he would. After all, Charley had passed the word out. *Everybody* would be there.

Pulcher went back to his apartment.

It was the first time he had surveyed his body since reclaiming it. The bathroom mirror told him that he had a gorgeous shiner indeed. Also certain twinges made him strip and examine his back. It looked, he thought gloomily, staring over his shoulder into the mirror, as though whoever had rented his body had had a perfectly marvelous time. He made a mental note to get a complete checkup some day soon, just in case. Then he showered, shaved, talcumed around the black eye without much success, and dressed.

He sat down, poured himself a drink and promptly forgot it was there. He was thinking. Something was trying to reach the surface of his mind. Something perfectly obvious, which he all the same couldn't quite put his finger on. It was rather annoying.

He found himself drowsily thinking of airfish.

Damn, he thought grouchily, his body's late tenant hadn't even troubled to give it a decent night's sleep! But he didn't want to sleep, not now. It was still only early evening. He supposed the Chester A. Arthur Day Dinner was still a must, but there were hours yet before that. . . .

He got up, poured the untasted drink into the sink and set out. There was one thing he could try to help Madeleine. It probably wouldn't work. But nothing else would either, so that was no reason for not trying it.

The mayor's mansion was ablaze with light; something was going on.

Pulcher trudged up the long, circling driveway in slush that kept splattering his ankles. He tapped gingerly on the door.

The butler took his name doubtfully, and isolated Pulcher in a contagion-free sitting room while he went off to see if the mayor would care to admit such a person. He came back looking incredulous. The mayor would.

Mayor Swinburne was a healthy, lean man of medium height, showing only by his thinning hair that he was in his middle forties. Pulcher said, "Mr. Mayor, I guess you know who I am. I represent the six kids who were accused of kidnaping your son."

"Not accused, Mr. Pulcher. Convicted. And I didn't know you still represented them."

"I see you know the score. All right. Maybe, in a legal sense, I don't represent them any more. But I'd like to make some representations on their behalf to you tonight—entirely unofficially." He gave the mayor a crisply worded, brief outline of what had happened in the case, how he had rented, what he had found as a renter, why he had missed the hearing. "You see, sir, the Tourist Agency doesn't give its renters even ordinary courtesy.

They're just bodies, nothing else. I can't blame those kids. Now that I've rented myself, I'll have to say that I wouldn't blame anybody who did *anything* to avoid it."

The mayor said dangerously, "Mr. Pulcher, I don't have to remind you that what's left of our economy depends heavily on the Tourist Agency for income. Also that some of our finest citizens are among its shareholders."

"Including yourself, Mr. Mayor. Right." Pulcher nodded. "But the management may not be reflecting your wishes. I'll go farther. I think, sir, that every contract the Tourist Agency holds with a renter ought to be voided as against public policy. Renting out your body for a purpose which well may be in violation of law—which, going by experience, nine times out of ten *does* involved a violation of law—is the same thing as contracting to perform any other illegal act. The contract simply cannot be enforced. The common law gives us a great many precedents on this point, and——"

"Please, Mr. Pulcher. I'm not a judge. If you feel so strongly, why not take it to court?"

Pulcher sank back into his chair, deflated. "There isn't time," he admitted. "And besides, it's too late for that to help the six persons I'm interested in. They've already been driven into an even more illegal act, in order to escape renting. I'm only trying to explain it to you, sir, because you are their only hope. You can pardon them."

The mayor's face turned beet red. "Executive clemency, from *me?* For *them?*"

"They didn't hurt your boy."

"No, they did not," the mayor agreed. "And I'm sure that Mrs. Gaultry, at least, would not willingly have done so. But can you say the same of the others? Could she have prevented it?" He stood up. "I'm sorry, Mr. Pulcher. The answer is no. Now you must excuse me."

Pulcher hesitated, then accepted the dismissal. There wasn't anything else to do.

He walked somberly down the hall toward the entrance, hardly noticing that guests were beginning to arrive. Apparently the mayor was offering cocktails to a select few. He recognized some of the faces—Lew Yoder, the County Tax Assessor for one; probably the mayor was having some of the whiter-collared politicians in for drinks before making the obligatory appearance at Dickon's fund-raising dinner. Pulcher looked up long enough to nod grayly at Yoder and walked on.

"Charley Dickon! What the devil are you doing here like that?"

Pulcher jerked upright. Dickon here? He looked around.

But Dickon was not in sight. Only Yoder was coming down the corridor toward him; oddly, Yoder was looking straight at him! And it had been Yoder's voice.

Yoder's face froze.

The expression on Yoder's face was an odd one but not unfamiliar to Milo Pulcher. He had seen it once before that day. It was the identical expression he had seen on the face of that young punk who had replaced him in court, Donley.

Yoder said awkwardly, "Oh, Milo, it's you. Hello. I, uh, thought you were Charley Dickon."

Pulcher felt the hairs at the back of his neck tingle. Something was odd here. Very odd. "It's a perfectly natural mistake," he said. "I'm six feet tall and Charley's five-feet three. I'm thirty-one years old. He's fifty. I'm dark and he's almost bald. I don't know how anybody ever tells us apart anyway."

"What the devil are you talking about?" Yoder blustered.

Pulcher looked at him thoughtfully for a second.

"You're lucky," he admitted. "I'm not sure I know. But I hope to find out."

V

Some things never change. Across the entrance to The New Metropolitan Cafe & Men's Grille a long scarlet banner carried the words:

VOTE THE STRAIGHT TICKET

Big poster portraits of the mayor and Committeeman Dickon flanked the door itself. A squat little soundtruck parked outside the door blared ancient marches of the sort that political conventions had suffered through for

more than two centuries back on Earth. It was an absolutely conventional political fund-raising dinner, it
would have the absolutely conventional embalmed
roast beef, the one conventionally free watery Manhattan at each place, and the conventionally boring after-
dinner speeches. (Except for one.) Milo Pulcher, stamping about in the slush outside the entrance, looked up at
the constellations visible from Altair Nine and wondered
if those same stars were looking down on just such another thousand dinners all over the Galaxy. Politics
went on, wherever you were. The constellations would
be different, of course; the Squirrel and the Nut were all
local stars and would have no shape at all from any other
system. But—

He caught sight of the tall thin figure he was waiting
for and stepped out into the stream of small-time political workers, ignoring their greetings. "Judge. I'm glad
you came."

Judge Pegrim said frostily, "I gave you my word,
Milo. But you've got a lot to answer to me for if this is a
false alarm. I don't ordinarily attend partisan political
affairs."

"It isn't an ordinary affair, judge." Pulcher conducted
him into the room and sat him at the table he had prepared. Once it had held place cards for four election-
board workers from the warehouse district, who now
buzzed from table to table angrily; Pulcher had filched
their cards. The judge was grumbling:

"It doesn't comport well with the bench to attend this
sort of thing, Milo. I don't like it."

"I know, Judge. You're an honest man. That's why I
wanted you here."

"Mmm." Pulcher left him before the *Mmm* could de-
velop into a question. He had fended off enough questions
since the thoughtful half hour he had spent pacing back
and forth in front of the mayor's mansion. He didn't
want to fend off any more. As he skirted the tables,
heading for the private room where he had left his
special guests, Charley Dickon caught his arm.

"Hey, Milo! I see you got the judge out. Good boy! He's
just what we needed to make this dinner complete."

"You have no idea how complete," said Pulcher pleasantly, and walked away. He didn't look back. There was another fine potential question-source; and the committeeman's would be even more difficult to answer than the judge's. Besides, he wanted to see Madeleine.

The girl and her five accomplices were where he had left them. The private bar where they were sitting was never used for affairs like this. You couldn't see the floor from it. Still, you could hear well enough, and that was more important.

The boys were showing nervousness in their separate ways. Although they had been convicted hardly more than a day, had been sentenced only a few hours, they had fallen quickly into the convict habit. Being out on bail so abruptly was a surprise. They hadn't expected it. It made them nervous. Young Foltis was jittering about, muttering to himself. The Hopgood boy was slumped despondently in a corner, blowing smoke rings. Jimmy Lasser was making a castle out of sugar cubes.

Only Madeleine was relaxed.

As Pulcher came in she looked up calmly. "Is everything all right?" He crossed his fingers and nodded. "Don't worry," she said. Pulcher blinked. *Don't worry.* It should have been he who was saying that to her, not the other way around. It came to him that there was only one possible reason for her calm confidence.

She trusted him.

But he couldn't stay. The ballroom was full now, and irritable banquet waiters were crashing plates down in front of the loyal Party workers. He had a couple of last-minute things to attend to. He carefully avoided the eye of Judge Pegrim, militantly alone at the table by the speaker's dais, and walked quickly across the room to Jimmy Lasser's father. He said without preamble: "Do you want to help your son?"

Tim Lasser snarled, "You cheap shyster! You wouldn't even show up for the trial! Where do you get the nerve to ask me a question like that?"

"Shut up. I asked you something."

Lasser hesitated, then read something in Pulcher's eyes. "Well, of course I do," he grumbled.

"Then tell me something. It won't sound important.

But it is. How many rifles did you sell in the past year?"

Lasser looked puzzled, but he said, "Not many. Maybe half a dozen. Business is lousy all over, you know, since the Icicle Works closed."

"And in a normal year?"

"Oh, three or four hundred. It's a big tourist item. You see, they need cold-shot rifles for hunting the fish. A regular bullet'll set them on fire—touches off the hydrogen. I'm the only sporting-goods merchant in town that carries them, and—say, what does that have to do with Jimmy?"

Pulcher took a deep breath. "Stick around and you'll find out. Meanwhile, think about what you just told me. If rifles are a tourist item, why did closing the Icicle Works hurt your sales?" He left.

But not quickly enough. Charley Dickon scuttled over and clutched his arm, his face furious. "Hey, Milo, what the hell! I just heard from Sam Apfel—the bondsman—that you got that whole bunch out of jail again on bail. How come?"

"They're my clients, Charley."

"Don't give me that! How'd you get them out when they're convicted, anyway?"

"I'm going to appeal the case," Pulcher said gently.

"You don't have a leg to stand on. Why would Pegrim grant bail anyhow?"

Pulcher pointed to Judge Pegrim's solitary table. "Ask him," he invited, and broke away.

He was burning a great many bridges behind him, he knew. It was an exhilarating feeling. Chancy but tingly; he decided he liked it. There was just one job to do. As soon as he was clear of the scowling but stopped committeeman, he walked by a circular route to the dais. Dickon was walking back to his table, turned away from the dais; Pulcher's chance would never be better. "Hello, Pop," he said.

Pop Craig looked up over his glasses. "Oh, Milo. I've been going over the list. You think I got everybody? Charley wanted me to introduce all the block captains and anybody else important. You know anybody important that ain't on this list?"

"That's what I wanted to tell you, Pop. Charley said

for you to give me a few minutes. I want to say a few words."

Craig said agitatedly, "Aw, Milo, if you make a speech they're all gonna want to make speeches! What do you want to make a speech for? You're no candidate."

Pulcher winked mysteriously. "What about next year?" he asked archly, with a lying inference.

"Oh. Oh-*ho*." Pop Craig nodded and returned to his list, mumbling. "Well. In *that* case. I guess I can fit you in after the block captains, or maybe after the man from the sheriff's office—" But Pulcher wasn't listening. Pulcher was already on his way back to the little private bar.

Man had conquered all of space within nearly fifty light years of dull, yellow old Sol, but out in that main ballroom political hacks were talking of long-dead presidents of almost forgotten countries centuries in the past. Pulcher was content to listen—to allow the sounds to vibrate his eardrums, at least, for the words made little sense to him. If, indeed, there was any content of sense to a political speech in the first place. But they were soothing.

Also they kept his six fledglings from bothering him with questions. Madeleine sat quietly by his shoulder, quite relaxed still and smelling faintly, pleasantly, of some floral aroma. It was, all in all, as pleasant a place to be as Pulcher could remember in his recent past. It was too bad that he would have to go out of it soon. . . .

Very soon.

The featured guest had droned through his platitudes. The visiting celebrities had said their few words each. Pop Craig's voluminous old voice took over again. "And now I wanta introduce some of the fine Party workers from our local districts. There's Keith Ciccarelli from the Hillside area. Keith, stand up and take a bow!" Dutiful applause. "And here's Mary Beth Whitehurst, head of the Women's Club from Riverview!" Dutiful applause—and a whistle. Surely the whistle was sardonic; Mary Beth was fat and would never again see fifty. There were more names.

Pulcher felt it coming the moment before Pop Craig reached his own name. He was on his way to the dais even before Craig droned out: "That fine young attorney and loyal Party man—the kind of young fellow our Party needs—Milo Pulcher!"

Dutiful applause again. That was habit, but Pulcher felt the whispering question that fluttered around the room.

He didn't give the question a chance to grow. He glanced once at the five hundred loyal Party faces staring up at him and began to speak. "Mr. President. Mr. Mayor. Justice Pegrim. Honored guests. Ladies and gentlemen." That was protocol. He paused. "What I have to say to you tonight is in the way of a compliment. It's a surprise for an old friend, sitting right here. That old friend is—Charley Dickon." He threw the name at them. It was a special political sort of delivery; a tone of voice that commanded: *Clap now.* They clapped. That was important, because it made it difficult for Charley to think of an excuse to interrupt him—as soon as Charley realized he ought to, which would be shortly.

"Way out here, on the bleak frontier of interstellar space, we live isolated lives, ladies and gentlemen." There were whispers, he could hear them. The words were more or less right, but he didn't have the right political accent; the audience knew there was something wrong. The true politician would have said: *This fine, growing frontier in the midst of interstellar space's greatest constellations.* He couldn't help it; he would have to rely on velocity now to get him through. "How isolated, we sometimes need to reflect. We have trade relations through the Icicle Works—now closed. We have tourists in both directions, through the Tourist Agency. We have ultrawave messages—also through the Tourist Agency. And that's about all.

"That's a very thin link, ladies and gentlemen. *Very* thin. And I'm here to tell you tonight that it would be even thinner if it weren't for my old friend there—yes, Committeeman Charley Dickon!" He punched the name again, and got the applause—but it was puzzled and died away early.

"The fact of the matter, ladies and gentlemen, is that just about every tourist that's come to Altair Nine this past year is the personal responsibility of Charley Dickon. Who have these tourists been? They haven't been businessmen—there's no business. They haven't been hunters. Ask Phil Lasser, over there; he hasn't sold enough fishing equipment to put in your eye. Ask yourselves, for that matter. How many of you have seen airfish right over the city? Do you know why? Because they aren't being hunted any more! There aren't any tourists to hunt them."

The time had come to give it to them straight. "The fact of the matter, ladies and gentlemen, is that the tourists we've had haven't been tourists at all. They've been natives, from right here on Altair Nine. Some of them are right in this room! I know that, because I rented myself for a few days—and do you know who took my body? Why, Charley did. Charley himself!" He was watching Lew Yoder out of the corner of his eye. The assessor's face turned gray; he seemed to shrink. Pulcher enjoyed the sight, though, after all, he had a certain debt to Lew Yoder; it was Yoder's slip of the tongue that had finally started him thinking on the right track. He went on hastily: "And what it all adds up to, ladies and gentlemen, is that Charley Dickon, and a handful of his friends in high places—most of them right here in this room— have cut off communication between Altair Nine and the rest of the Galaxy!"

That did it.

There were yells, and the loudest yell came from Charley Dickon. "Throw him out! Arrest him! Craig, get the sergeant-at-arms! I say I don't have to sit here and listen to this maniac!"

"*And I say you do*," boomed the cold courtroom voice of Judge Pegrim. The judge stood up. "Go on, Pulcher!" he ordered. "I came here tonight to hear what you have to say. It may be wrong. It may be right. I propose to hear all of it before I make up my mind."

Thank heaven for the cold old judge! Pulcher cut right in before Dickon could find a new point of attack; there wasn't much left to say anyway. "The story is simple, ladies and gentlemen. The Icicle Works was the most profitable corporation in the Galaxy. We all know that.

Probably everybody in this room had a couple of shares of stock. Dickon had plenty.

"But he wanted more. And he didn't want to pay for them. So he used his connection with the Tourist Agency to cut off communication between Nine and the rest of the Galaxy. He spread the word that Altamycin was worthless now because some fictitious character had invented a cheap new substitute. He closed down the Icicle Works. And for the last twelve months he's been picking up stock for a penny on the dollar, while the rest of us starve and the Altamycin the rest of the Galaxy needs stays right here on Altair Nine and—"

He stopped, not because he had run out of words but because no one could hear them any longer. The noises the crowd was making were no longer puzzled, they were ferocious. It figured. Apart from Dickon's immediate gang of manipulators, there was hardly a man in the room who hadn't taken a serious loss in the past year.

It was time for the police to come rushing in, as per the phone call Judge Pegrim had made, protestingly, when Pulcher urged him to the dinner. They did—just barely in time. They weren't needed to arrest Dickon so much; but they were indispensable for keeping him from being lynched.

Hours later, escorting Madeleine home, Milo was still bubbling over. "I was worried about the Mayor! I couldn't make up my mind whether he was in it with Charley or not. I'm glad he wasn't, because he said he owed me a favor, and I told him how he could pay it. Executive clemency. The six of you will be free in the morning."

Madeleine said sleepily, "I'm free enough now."

"And the Tourist Agency won't be able to enforce those contracts any more. I talked it over with Judge Pegrim. He wouldn't give me an official statement, but he said—Madeleine, you're not listening."

She yawned. "It's been an exhausting day, Milo," she apologized. "Anyway, you can tell me all about that later. We'll have plenty of time."

"Years and years," he promised. "Years and—" They

stopped talking. The mechanical cab-driver, sneaking around through back streets to avoid the resentment of displaced live drivers, glanced over its condenser cells at them and chuckled, making tiny sparks in the night.

CPSIA information can be obtained
at www.ICGtesting.com
Printed in the USA
BVOW08s2301120717
489208BV00014B/159/P